FOR ORGANS, PIANOS & ELECTRONIC KEYBOARDS

E-Z PLAY TODAY
116

SONGS FROM
A STAR IS BORN • LA LA LAND
THE GREATEST SHOWMAN

AND MORE
MOVIE MUSICALS
20 SONGS FROM 8 HIT MOVIES

ISBN 978-1-5400-4395-5

E-Z Play® Today Music Notation © 1975 by HAL LEONARD LLC
E-Z PLAY and EASY ELECTRONIC KEYBOARD MUSIC are registered trademarks of HAL LEONARD LLC.

Visit Hal Leonard Online at
www.halleonard.com

Contact us:
Hal Leonard
7777 West Bluemound Road
Milwaukee, WI 53213
Email: info@halleonard.com

In Europe, contact:
Hal Leonard Europe Limited
42 Wigmore Street
Marylebone, London, W1U 2RN
Email: info@halleonardeurope.com

In Australia, contact:
Hal Leonard Australia Pty. Ltd.
4 Lentara Court
Cheltenham, Victo
Email: info@halleo

Aug 2019

Registration Guide

- Match the Registration number on the song to the corresponding numbered category below. Select and activate an instrumental sound available on your instrument.

- Choose an automatic rhythm appropriate to the mood and style of the song. (Consult your Owner's Guide for proper operation of automatic rhythm features.)

- Adjust the tempo and volume controls to comfortable settings.

Registration

1	Mellow	Flutes, Clarinet, Oboe, Flugel Horn, Trombone, French Horn, Organ Flutes
2	Ensemble	Brass Section, Sax Section, Wind Ensemble, Full Organ, Theater Organ
3	Strings	Violin, Viola, Cello, Fiddle, String Ensemble, Pizzicato, Organ Strings
4	Guitars	Acoustic/Electric Guitars, Banjo, Mandolin, Dulcimer, Ukulele, Hawaiian Guitar
5	Mallets	Vibraphone, Marimba, Xylophone, Steel Drums, Bells, Celesta, Chimes
6	Liturgical	Pipe Organ, Hand Bells, Vocal Ensemble, Choir, Organ Flutes
7	Bright	Saxophones, Trumpet, Mute Trumpet, Synth Leads, Jazz/Gospel Organs
8	Piano	Piano, Electric Piano, Honky Tonk Piano, Harpsichord, Clavi
9	Novelty	Melodic Percussion, Wah Trumpet, Synth, Whistle, Kazoo, Perc. Organ
10	Bellows	Accordion, French Accordion, Mussette, Harmonica, Pump Organ, Bagpipes

Tomorrow
from the Musical Production ANNIE

Registration 1
Rhythm: Swing or Jazz

Lyric by Martin Charnin
Music by Charles Strouse

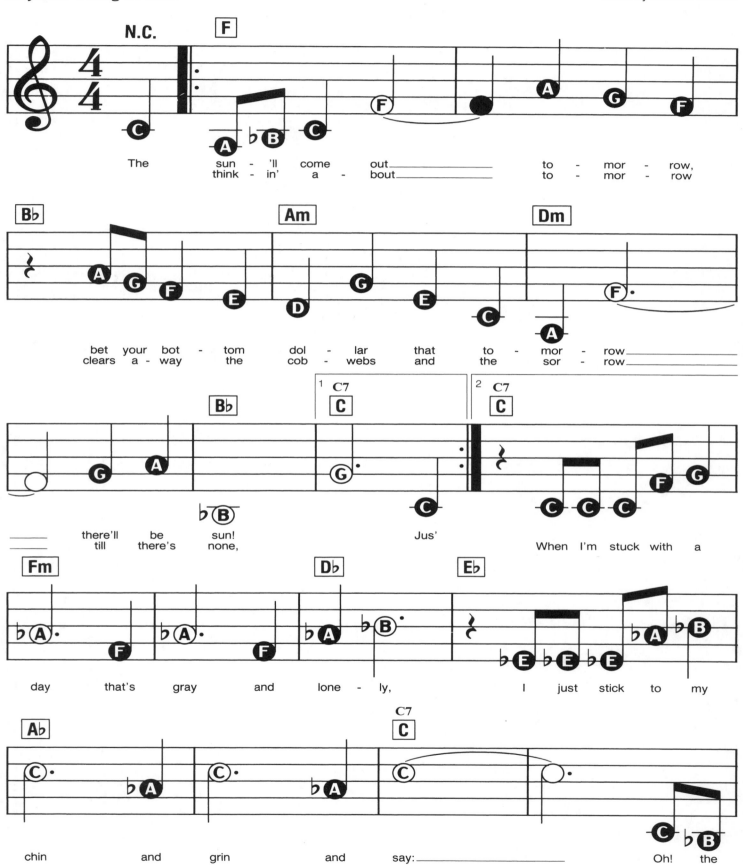

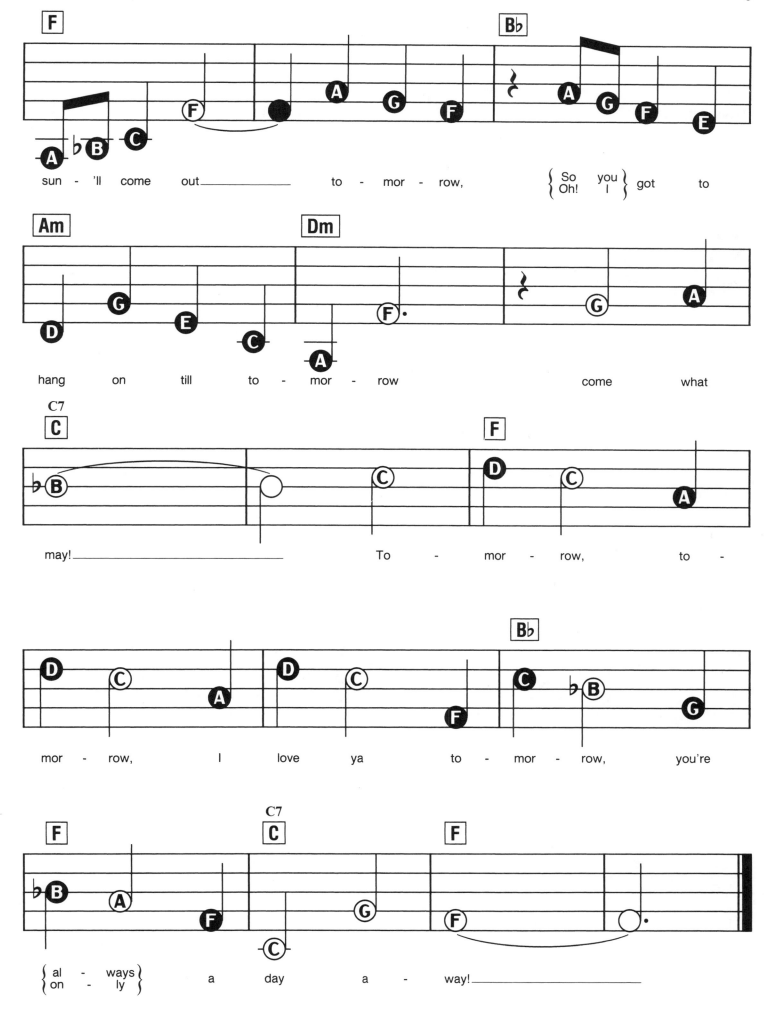

Evermore
from BEAUTY AND THE BEAST

Registration 2
Rhythm: Ballad

Music by Alan Menken
Lyrics by Tim Rice

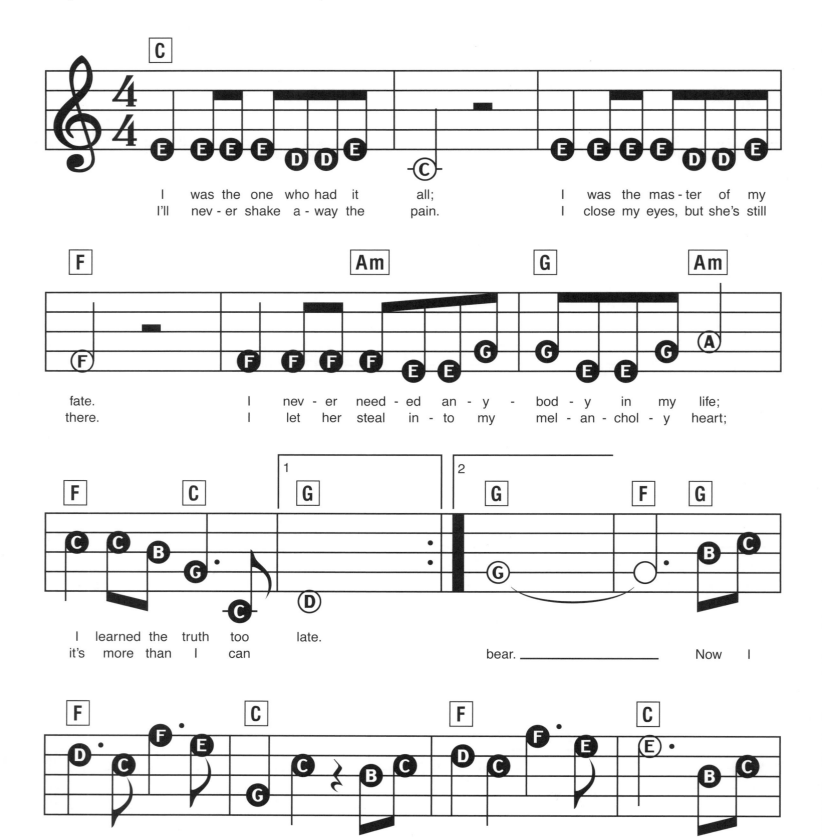

I was the one who had it all;
I'll nev - er shake a - way the pain.
I was the mas - ter of my
I close my eyes, but she's still

fate.
there.
I nev - er need - ed an - y - bod - y in my life;
I let her steal in - to my mel - an - chol - y heart;

I learned the truth too late.
it's more than I can bear. _____ Now I

know she'll nev - er leave me, e - ven as she runs a - way. She will

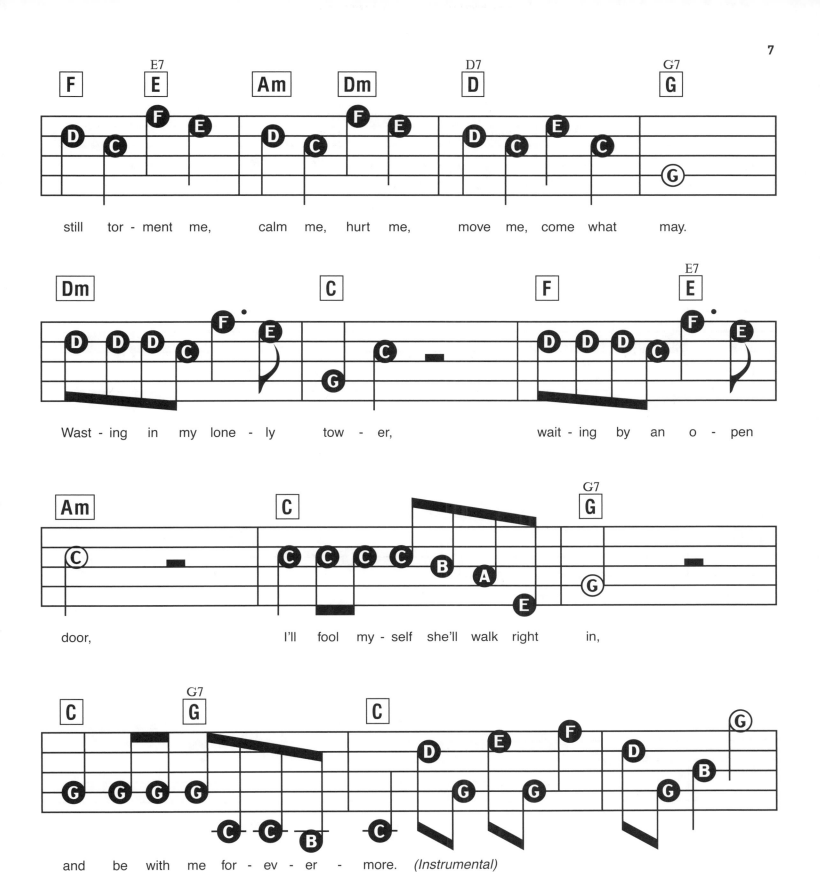

still tor - ment me, calm me, hurt me, move me, come what may.

Wast - ing in my lone - ly tow - er, wait - ing by an o - pen

door, I'll fool my - self she'll walk right in,

and be with me for - ev - er - more. *(Instrumental)*

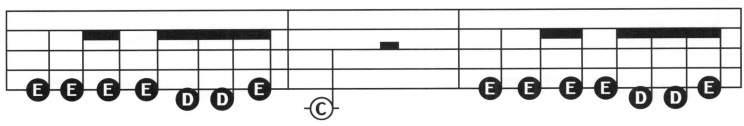

I rage a - gainst the trials of love. I curse the fad - ing of the

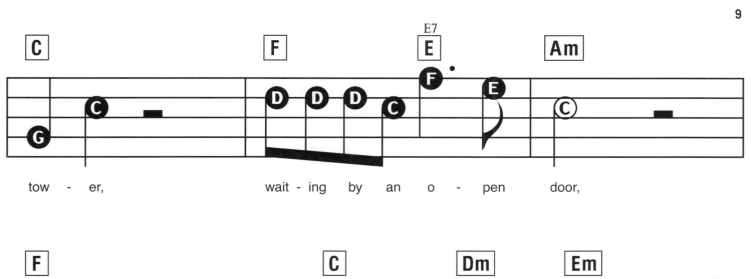

tow - er,   wait - ing by an o - pen door,

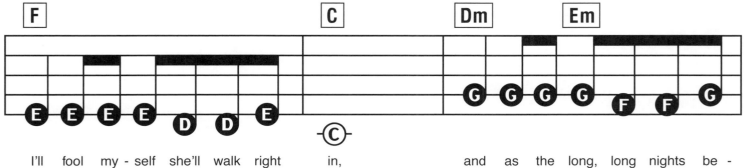

I'll fool my - self she'll walk right in,   and as the long, long nights be -

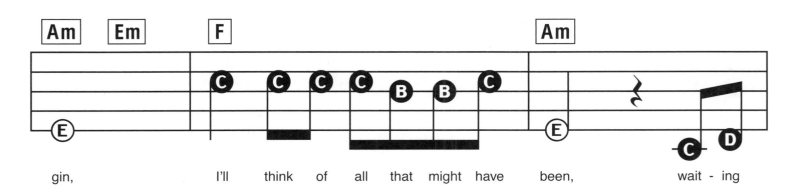

gin,   I'll think of all that might have been,   wait - ing

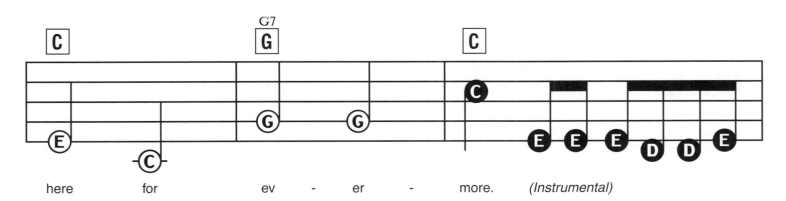

here   for   ev - er - more. *(Instrumental)*

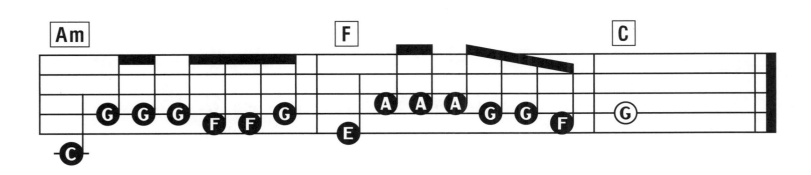

How Does a Moment Last Forever
from BEAUTY AND THE BEAST

Registration 1
Rhythm: Broadway or Ballad

Music by Alan Menken
Lyrics by Tim Rice

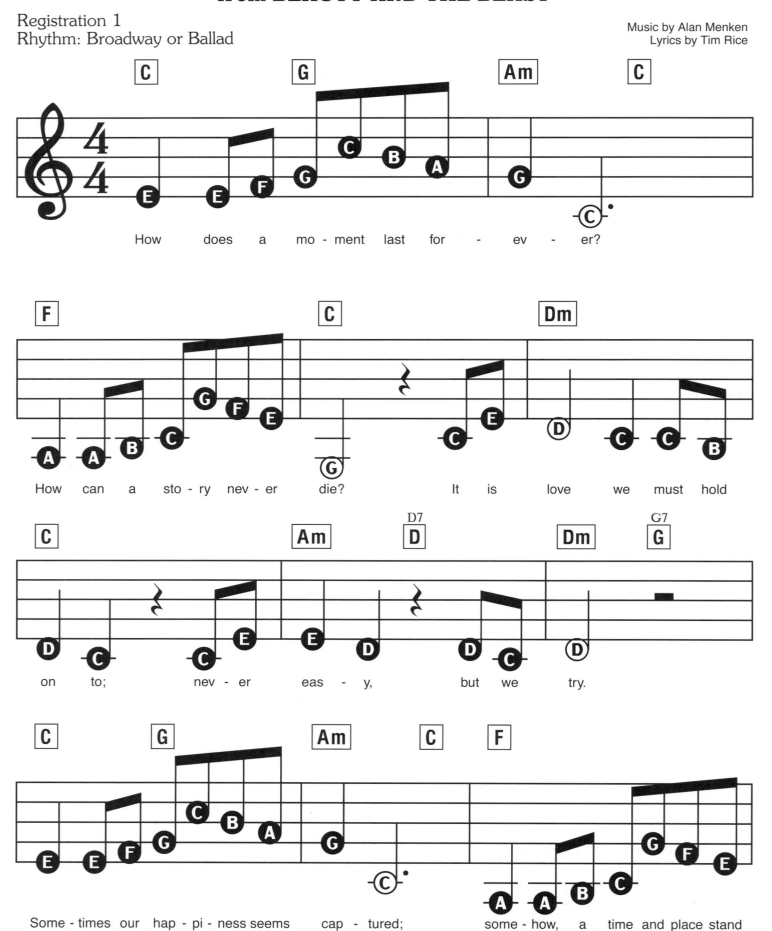

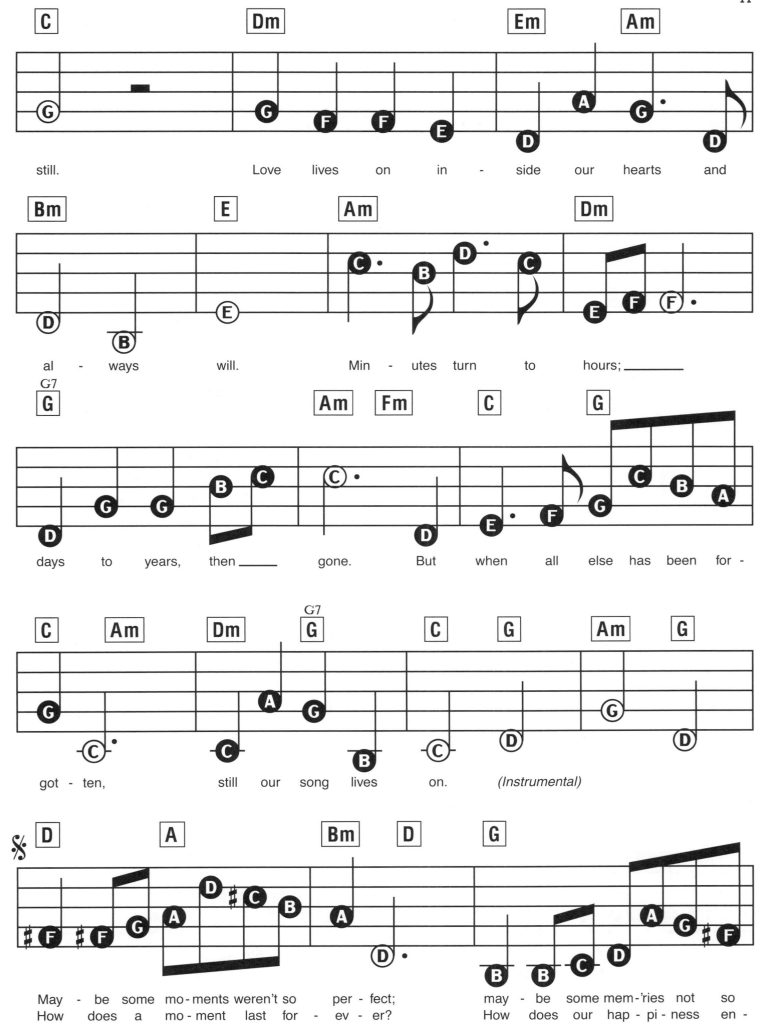

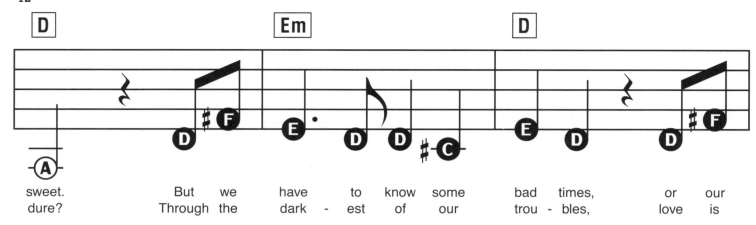

sweet. But we have to know some bad times, or our
dure? Through the dark - est of our trou - bles, love is

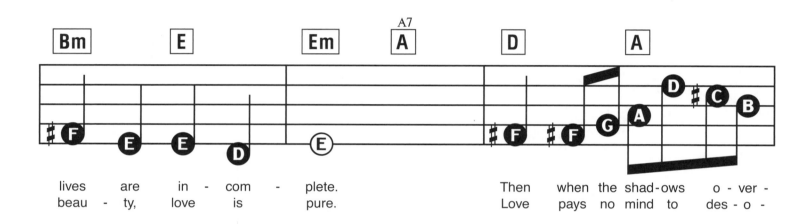

lives are in - com - plete. Then when the shad - ows o - ver -
beau - ty, love is pure. Love pays no mind to des - o -

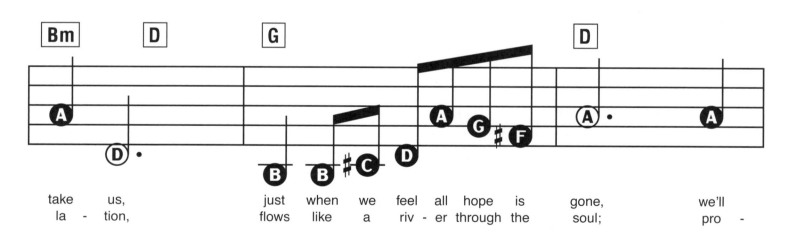

take us, just when we feel all hope is gone, we'll
la - tion, flows like a riv - er through the soul; pro -

To Coda ⊕

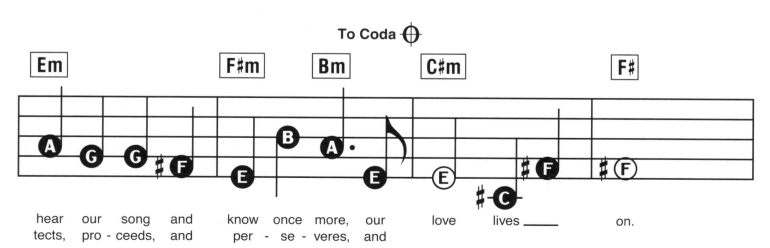

hear our song and know once more, our love lives ____ on.
tects, pro - ceeds, and per - se - veres, and

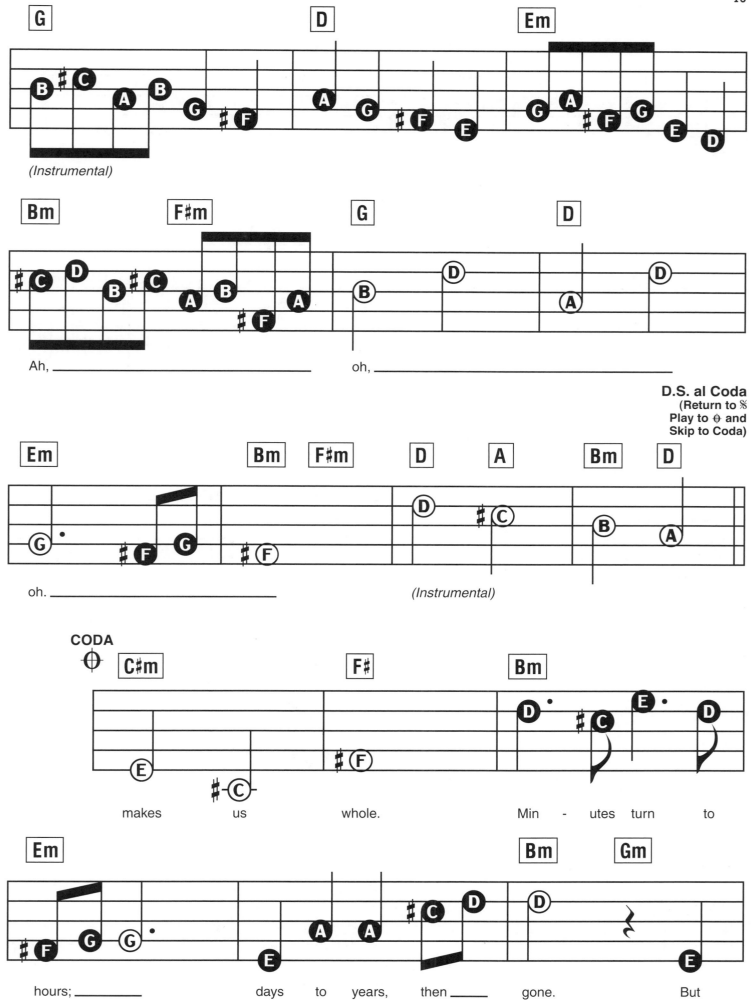

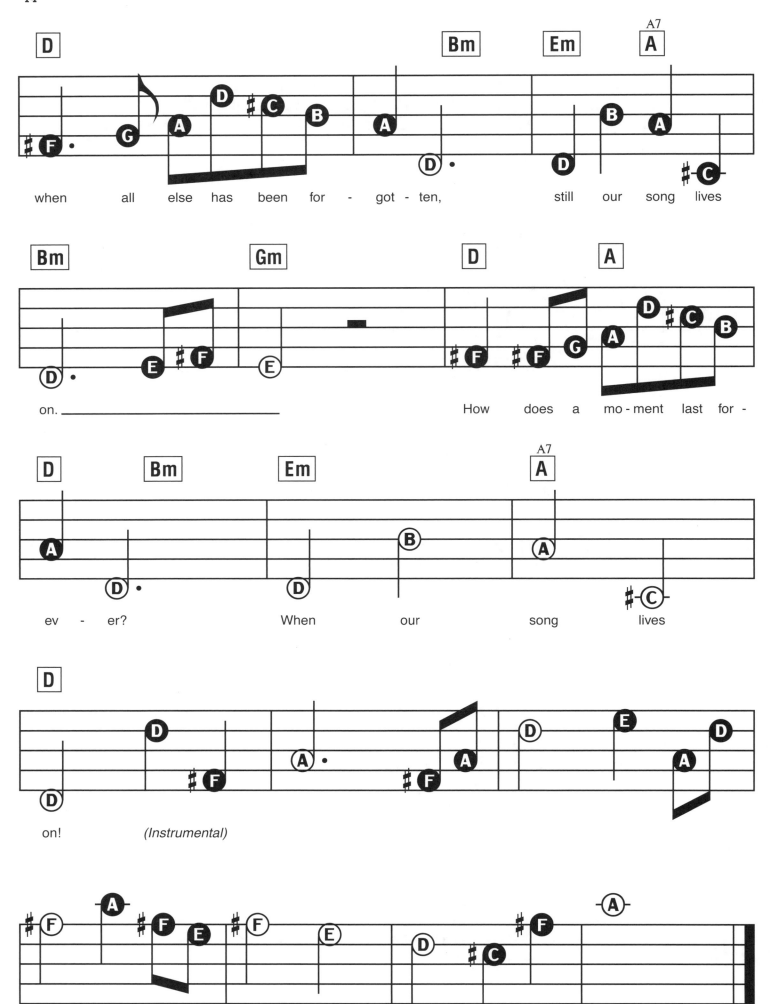

when all else has been for - got - ten, still our song lives on.

How does a mo - ment last for - ev - er? When our song lives on!

(Instrumental)

This Is Me
from THE GREATEST SHOWMAN

Registration 1
Rhythm: None

Words and Music by Benj Pasek
and Justin Paul

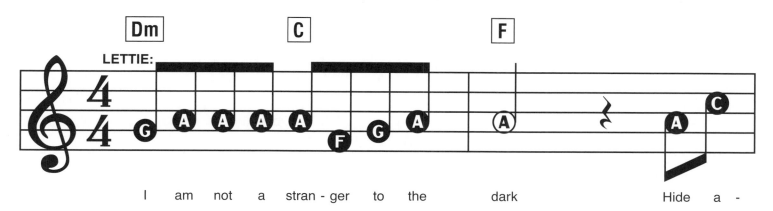

I am not a stran-ger to the dark   Hide a -

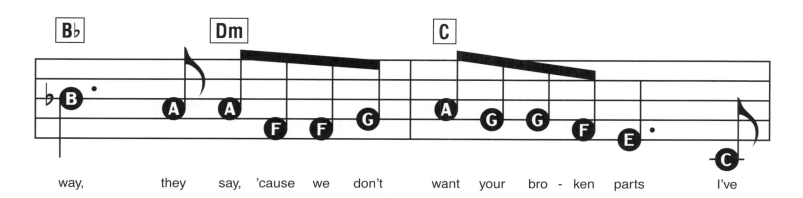

way, they say, 'cause we don't want your bro-ken parts   I've

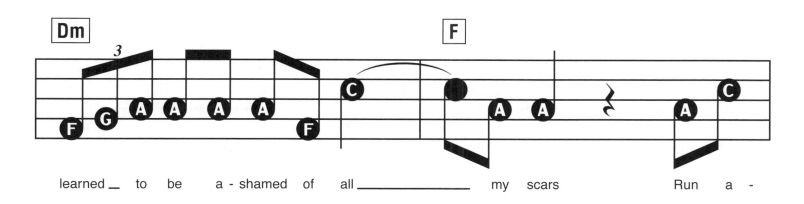

learned __ to be a-shamed of all _____ my scars   Run a -

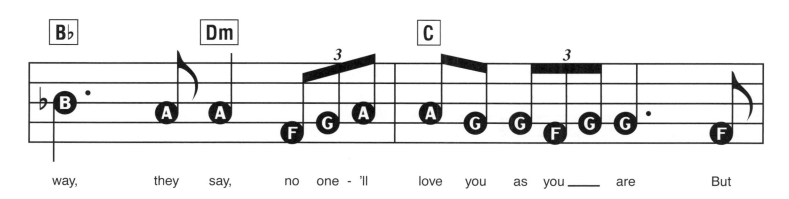

way, they say,   no one-'ll love you as you __ are   But

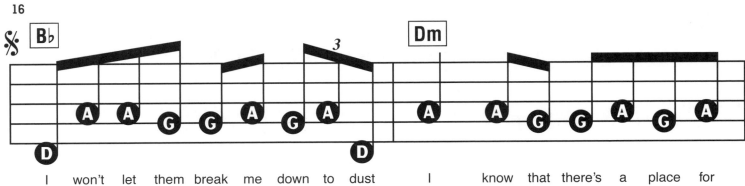

I won't let them break me down to dust I know that there's a place for

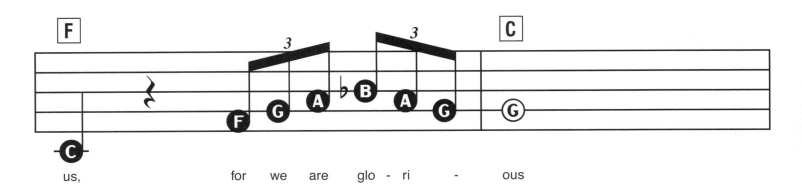

us, for we are glo - ri - ous

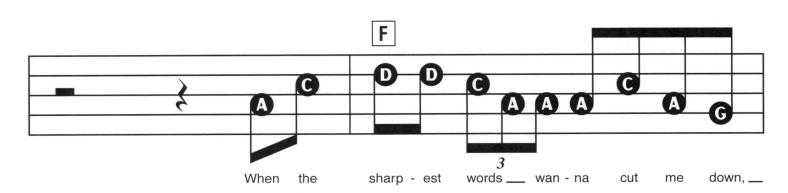

When the sharp - est words __ wan - na cut me down, __

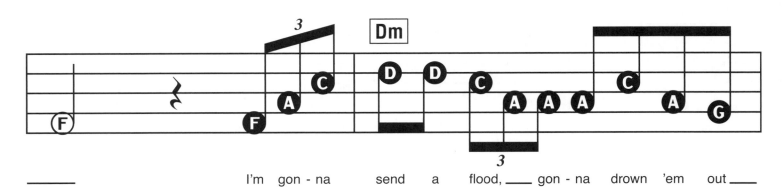

__ I'm gon - na send a flood, __ gon - na drown 'em out __

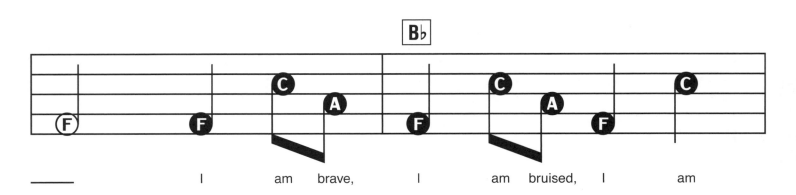

__ I am brave, I am bruised, I am

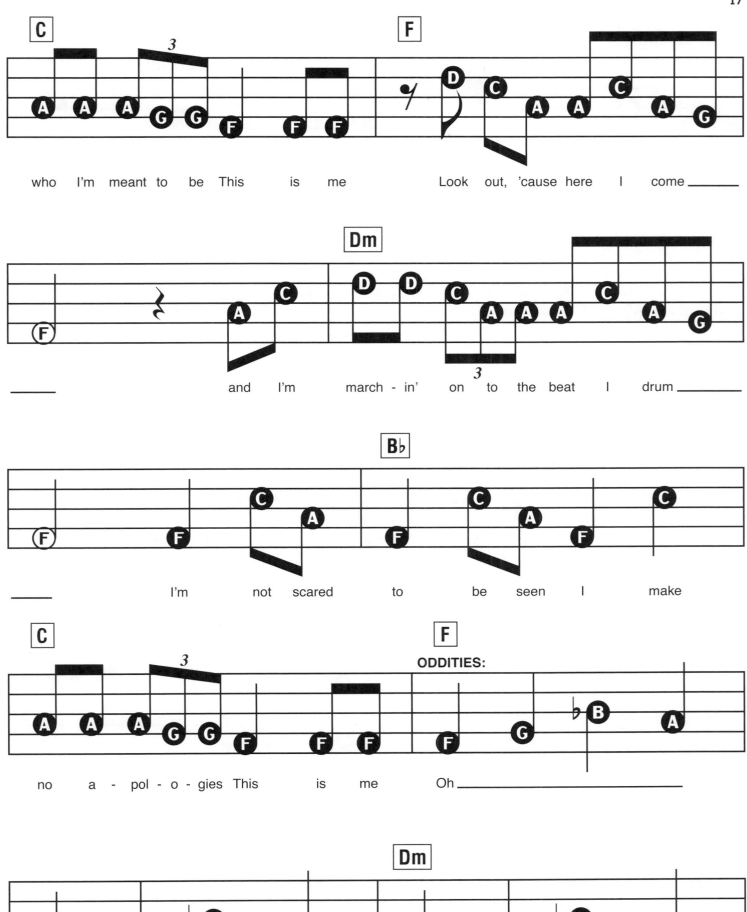

who I'm meant to be This is me   Look out, 'cause here I come _____

_____   and I'm march - in' on to the beat I drum _____

_____   I'm   not scared   to   be seen I   make

no a - pol - o - gies This   is   me   Oh _____

Oh _____   Oh _____

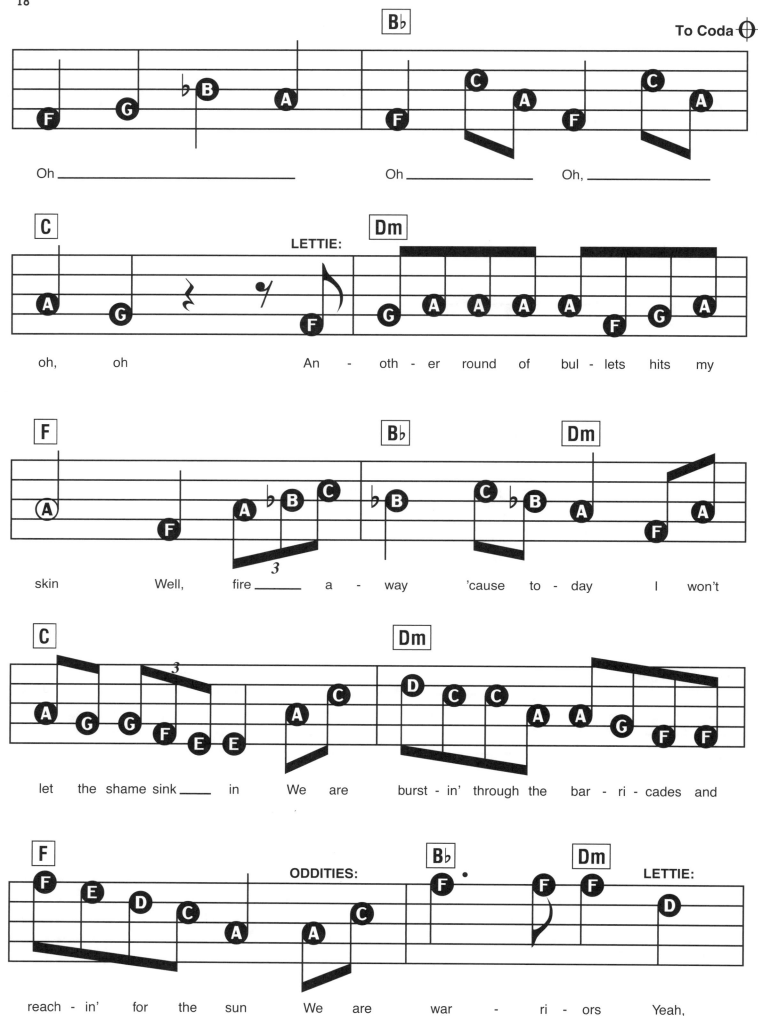

To Coda

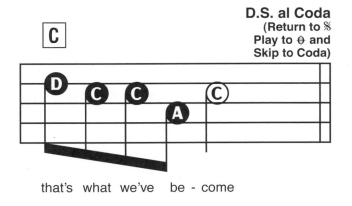

that's what we've be - come

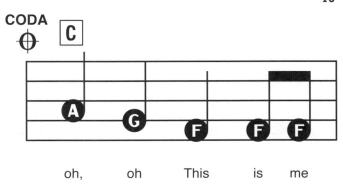

oh,   oh   This   is   me

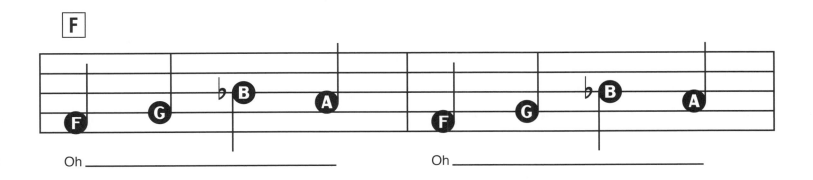

Oh _____   Oh _____

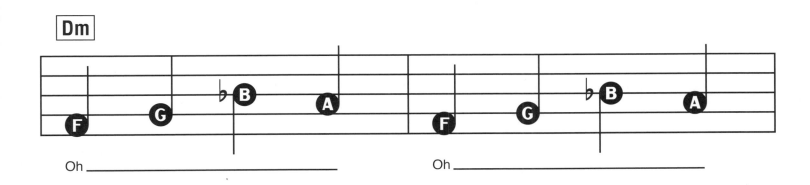

Oh _____   Oh _____

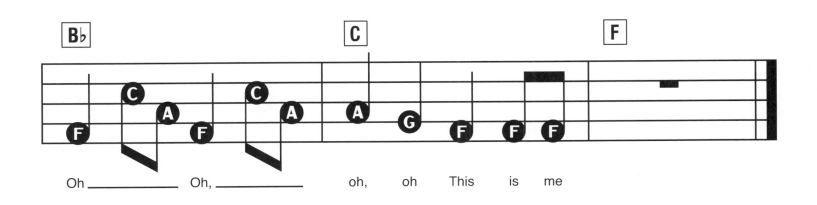

Oh _____ Oh, _____   oh,   oh This   is   me

A Million Dreams
from THE GREATEST SHOWMAN

Registration 2
Rhythm: Broadway or Show Tunes

Words and Music by Benj Pasek
and Justin Paul

YOUNG BARNUM:

I close my eyes and I can see a world that's
There's a house we can build

wait - ing up for me that I call my
room in - side is filled with things from my

own (Instrumental) Through the
a - way Spe - cial

dark, through the door, through where no one's been be -
things I com - pile, each one there to make you

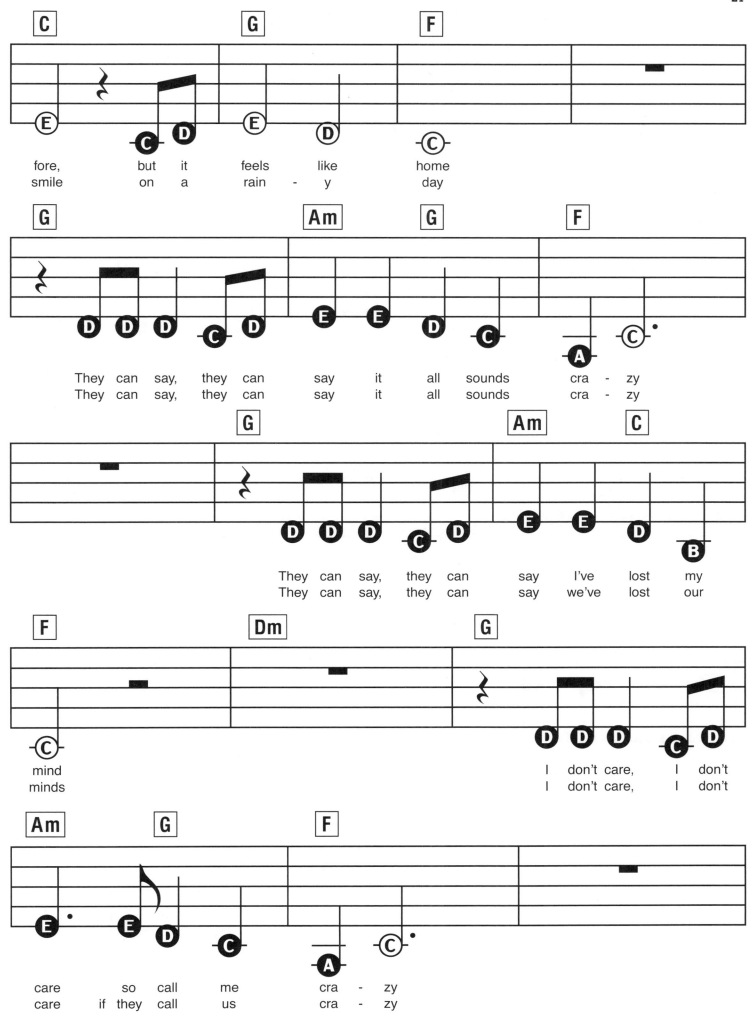

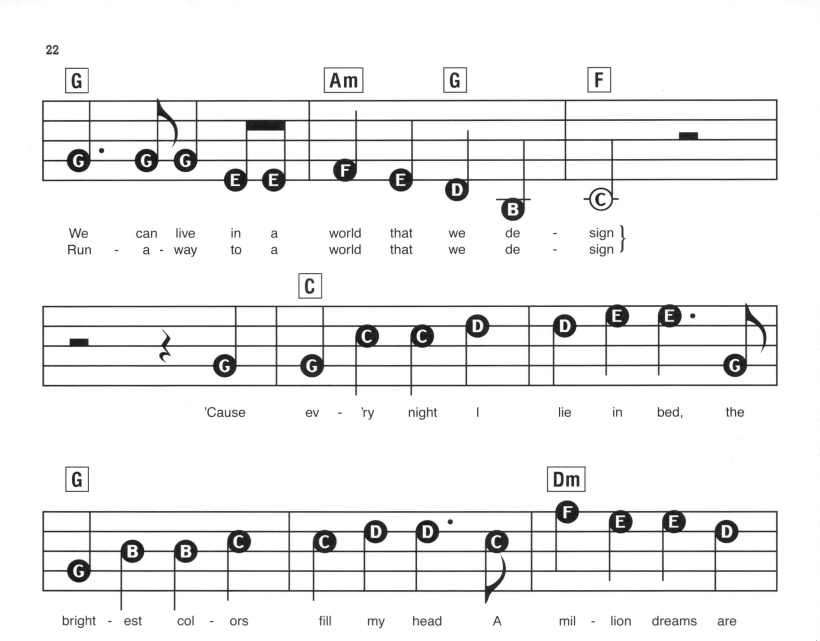

C G F
fore, but it feels like home
smile on a rain - y day
G Am G F
They can say, they can say it all sounds cra - zy
They can say, they can say it all sounds cra - zy
G Am C
They can say, they can say I've lost my
They can say, they can say we've lost our
F Dm G
mind I don't care, I don't
minds I don't care, I don't
Am G F
care so call me cra - zy
care if they call us cra - zy

We can live in a world that we de - sign
Run - a - way to a world that we de - sign

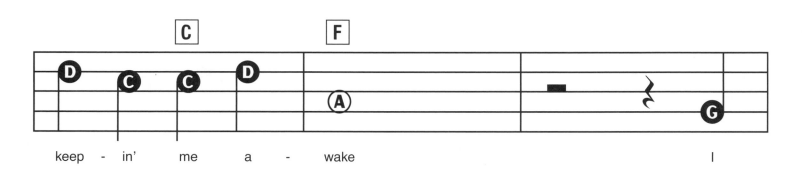

'Cause ev - 'ry night I lie in bed, the

bright - est col - ors fill my head A mil - lion dreams are

keep - in' me a - wake I

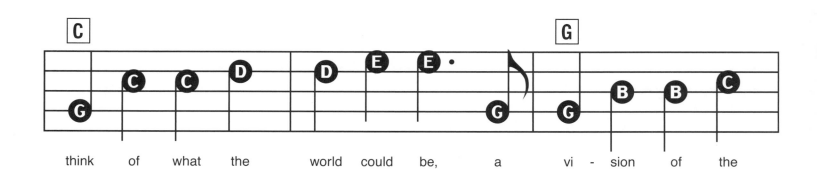

think of what the world could be, a vi - sion of the

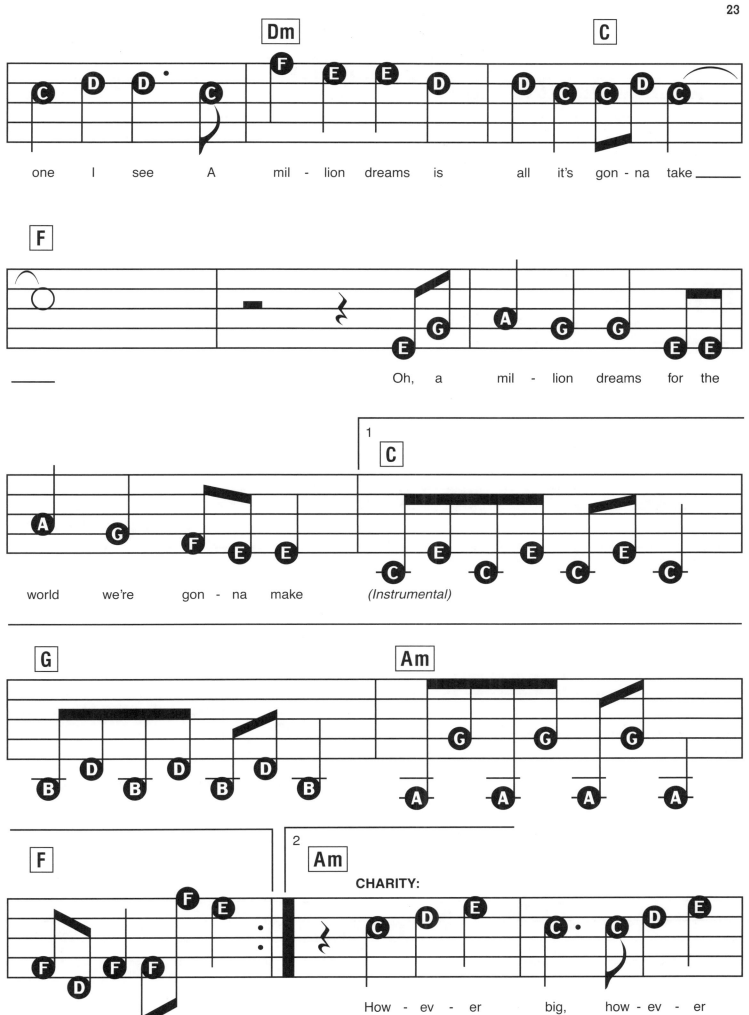

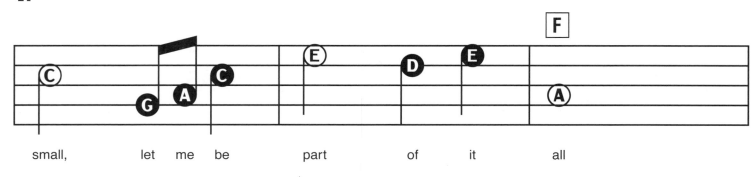

small,   let me be   part   of   it   all

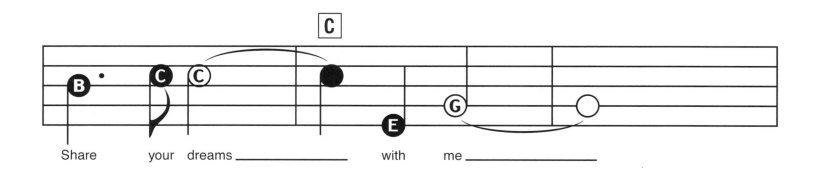

Share   your dreams _____ with   me _____

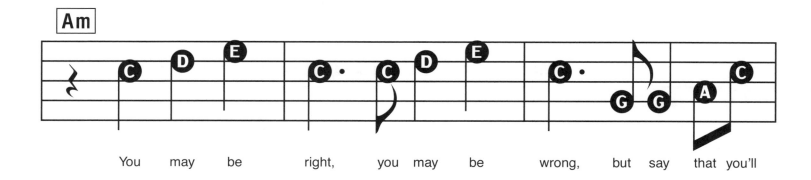

You   may   be   right,   you   may   be   wrong,   but say   that you'll

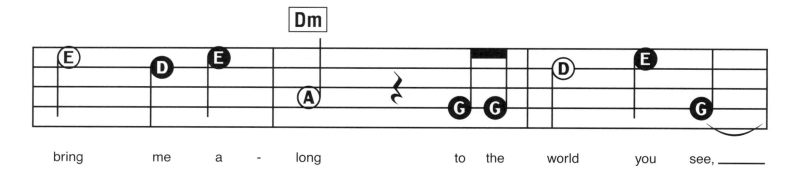

bring   me   a - long   to the world you see, _____

BARNUM & CHARITY:

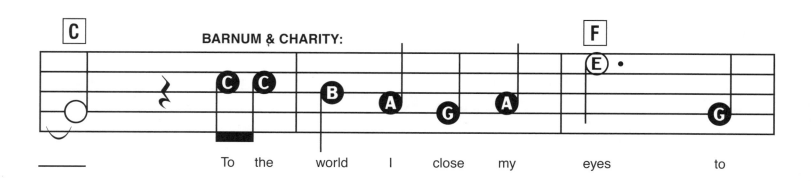

_____ To the world I   close my   eyes   to

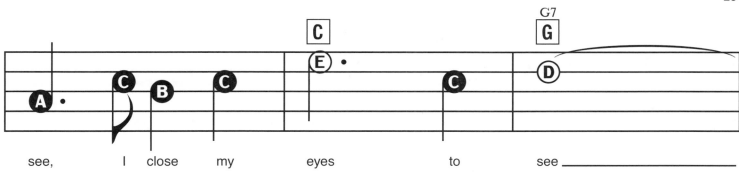

see,	I	close	my	eyes	to	see _____

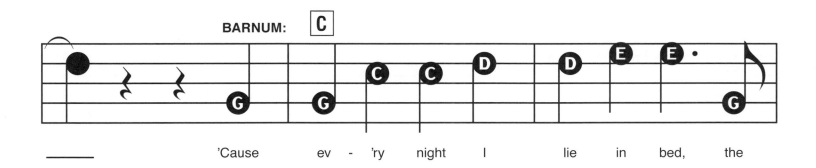

____	'Cause	ev - 'ry	night	I	lie	in	bed,	the

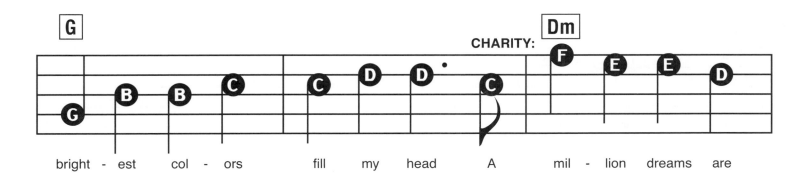

bright - est	col - ors	fill	my	head	A	mil - lion	dreams	are

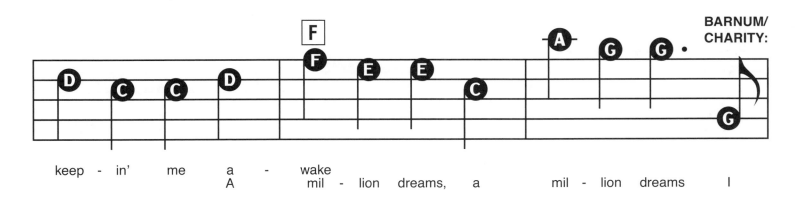

keep - in' me	a - wake
A	mil - lion	dreams,	a	mil - lion	dreams	I

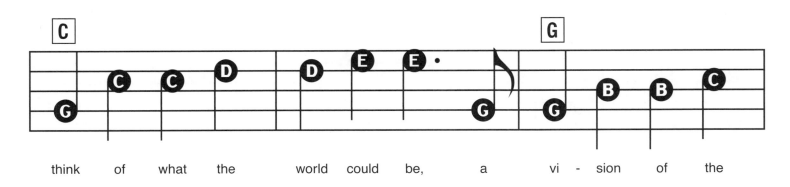

think	of	what	the	world	could	be,	a	vi - sion	of	the

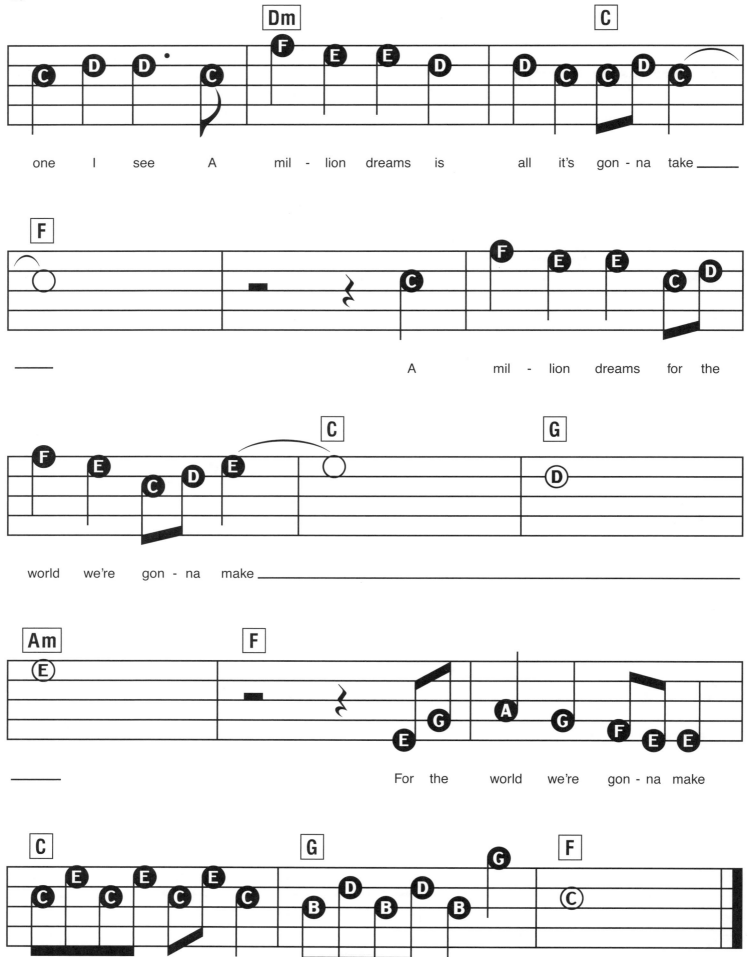

one I see A mil - lion dreams is all it's gon - na take _____

_____ A mil - lion dreams for the

world we're gon - na make _____

_____ For the world we're gon - na make

(Instrumental)

Suddenly
from LES MISÉRABLES

Registration 3
Rhythm: Ballad

Music by Claude-Michel Schonberg
Lyrics by Herbert Kretzmer and Alain Boublil

Sud - den - ly you're here, sud - den - ly it starts.
Sud - den - ly the world seems a diff - 'rent place,

Can two anx - ious hearts beat as one?
some - how full of grace, full of light.

Yes - ter - day I was a - lone, to - day you are be - side me.
How was I to know that so much hope was held in - side me?

Some - thing still un - clear, some - thing not yet here has be -
What is past, is gone. Now we jour - ney on through the

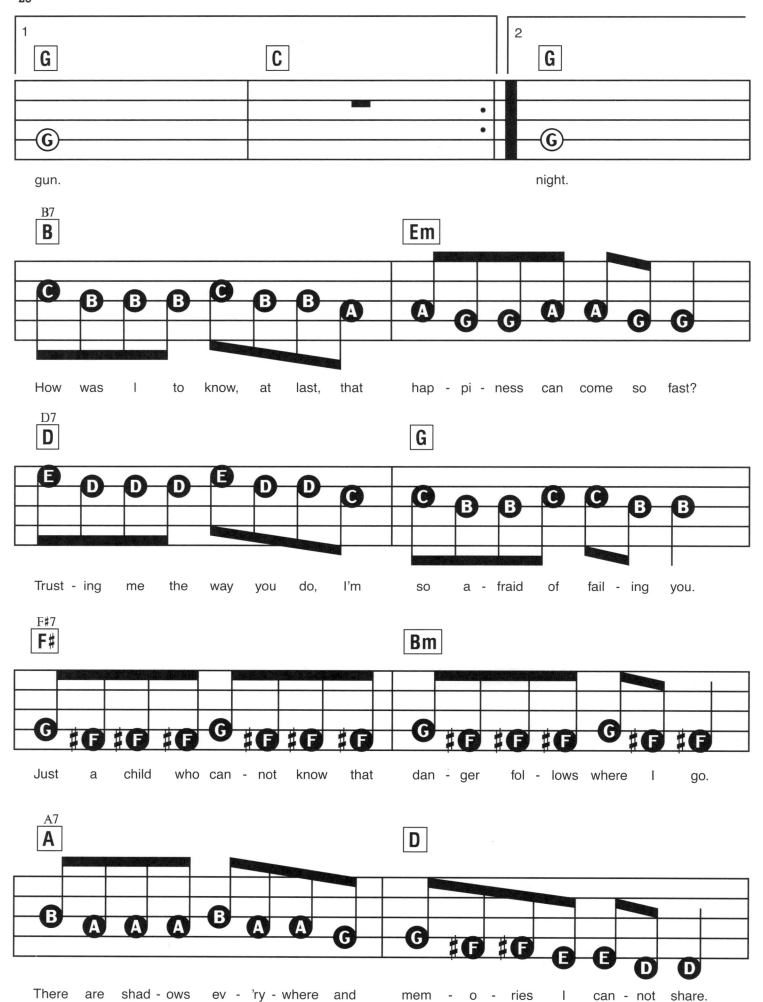

gun.

night.

How was I to know, at last, that hap - pi - ness can come so fast?

Trust - ing me the way you do, I'm so a - fraid of fail - ing you.

Just a child who can - not know that dan - ger fol - lows where I go.

There are shad - ows ev - 'ry - where and mem - o - ries I can - not share.

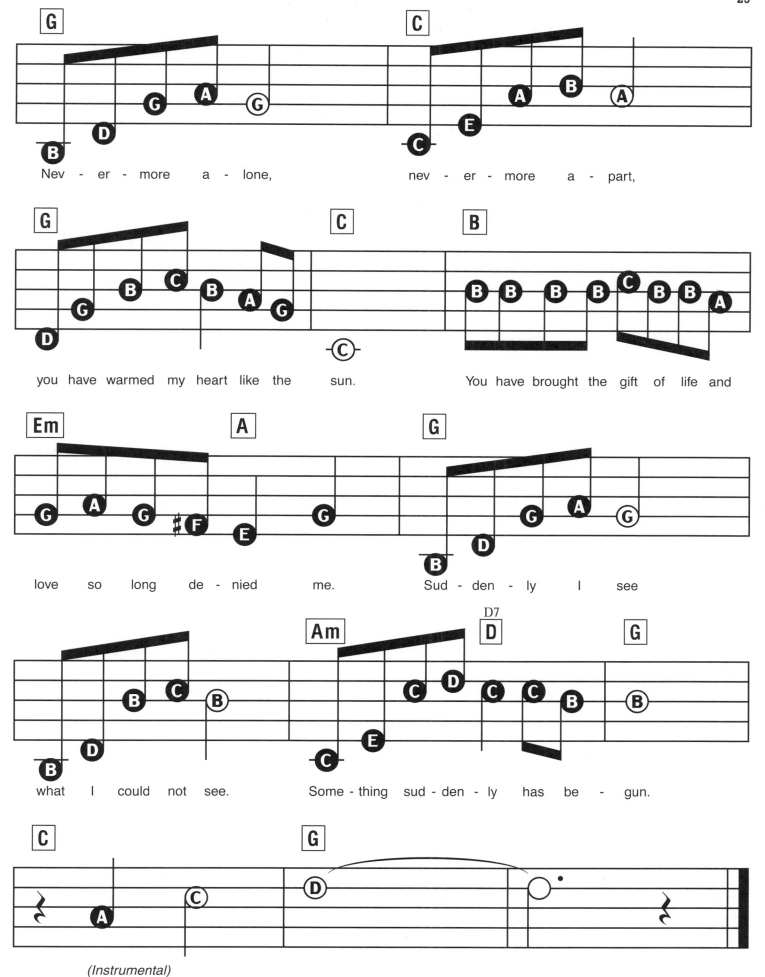

Nev - er - more a - lone, nev - er - more a - part,

you have warmed my heart like the sun. You have brought the gift of life and

love so long de - nied me. Sud - den - ly I see

what I could not see. Some - thing sud - den - ly has be - gun.

(Instrumental)

On the Steps of the Palace
(Film Version)
from INTO THE WOODS

Registration 8
Rhythm: None

Words and Music by
Stephen Sondheim

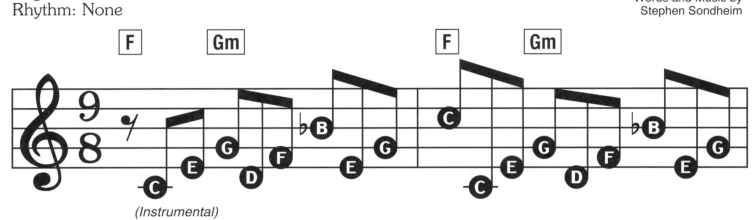

(Instrumental)

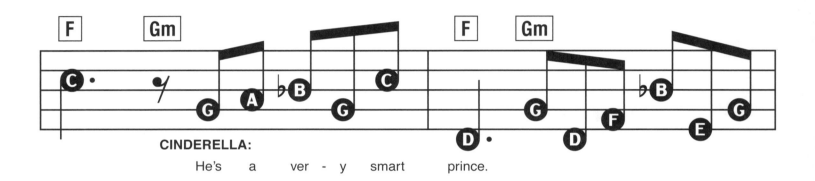

CINDERELLA:

He's a ver - y smart prince.

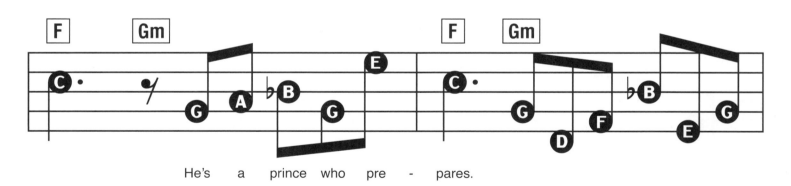

He's a prince who pre - pares.

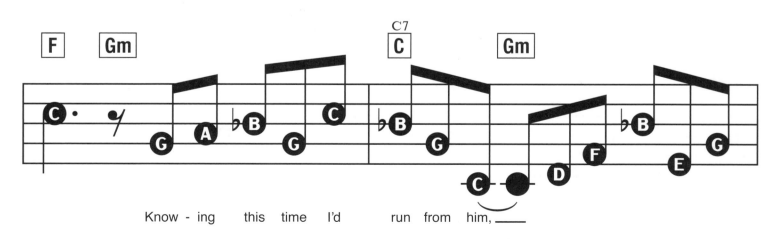

Know - ing this time I'd run from him, _____

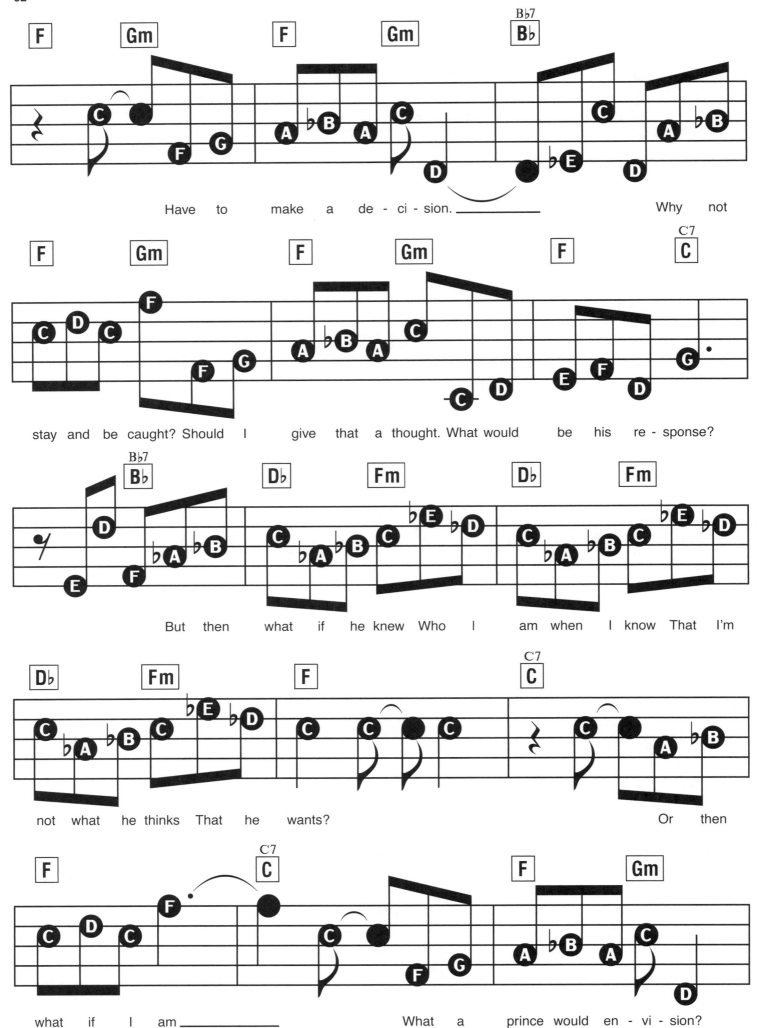

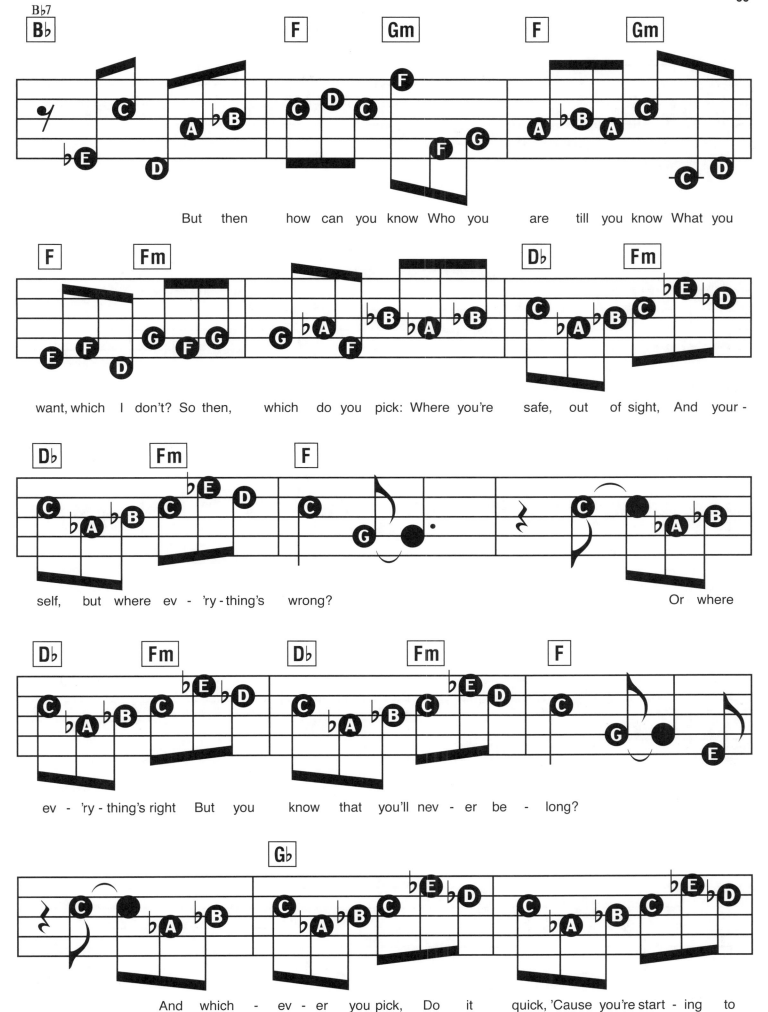

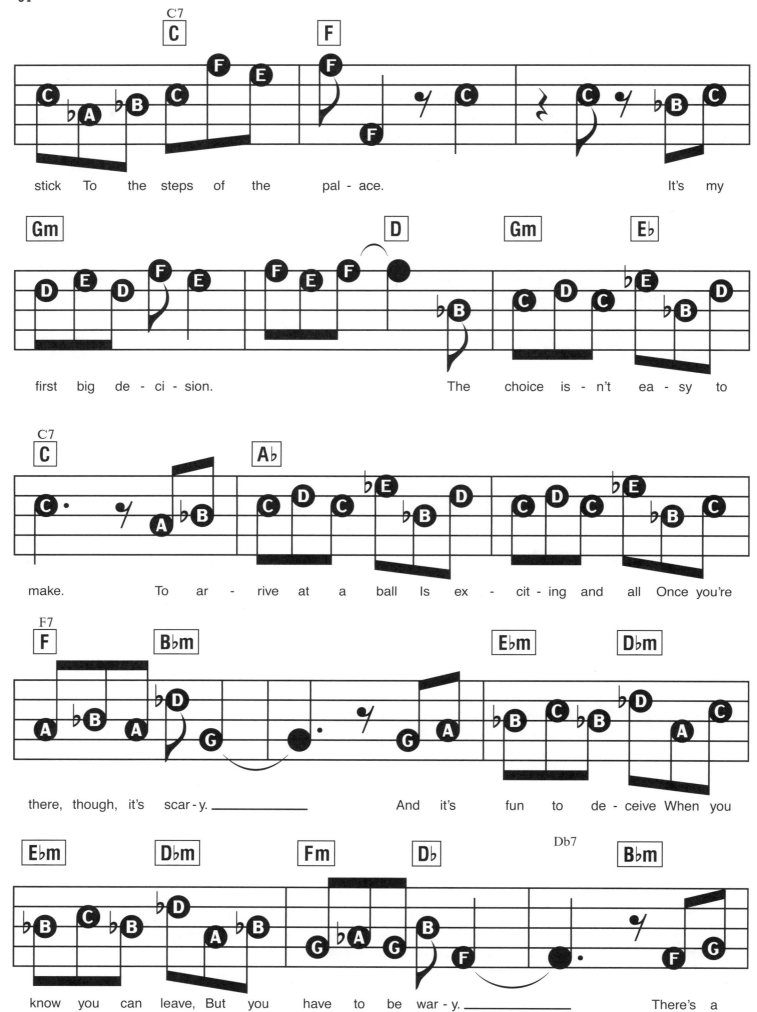

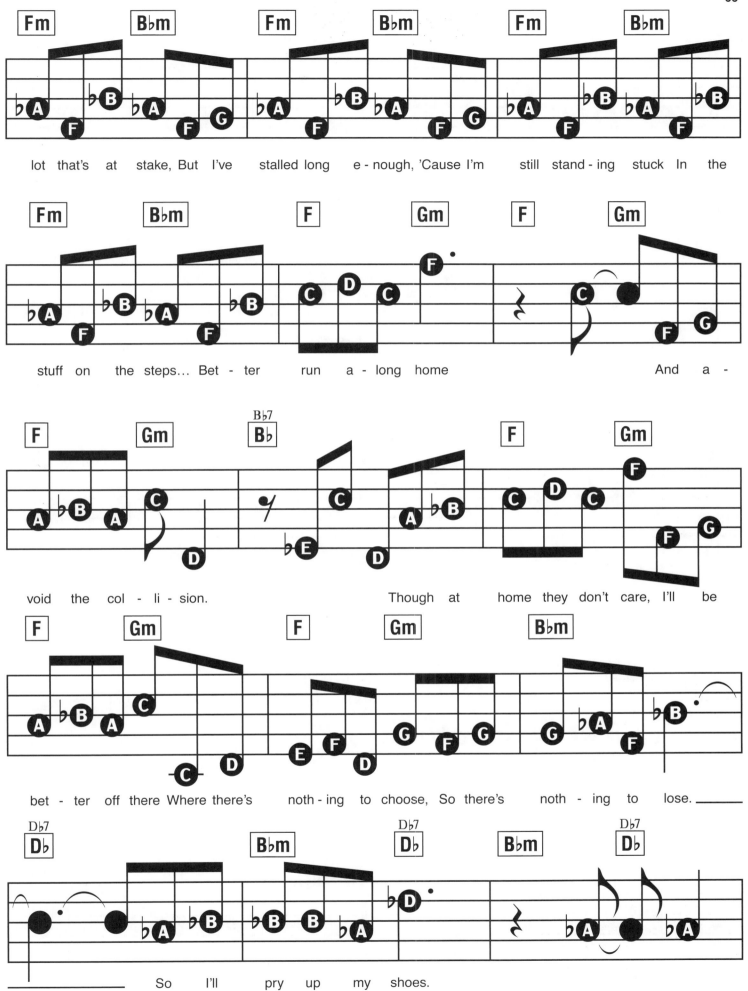

Bbm / Db7 Db / F / Gm / F / Gm

Wait, though, think - ing it through, Things don't

F / Gm / F / Gm / Am

have to col - lide I know what my de - ci - sion is,

Gm / Am / Gm / Am / Gm / Am

Which is not to de - cide. I'll just leave him a

Gm / Am / Gm / Am / Gm / Am

clue: For ex - am - ple, a shoe.

Gm / Am / Gm / Am / Gm / Am

And then see what he'll do. Now it's he and not

you Who'll be stuck with a shoe In a stew,

In the goo, And I've

learned some - thing too, Some - thing I nev - er knew, _____

On the steps of the pal - ace! _____

Audition
(The Fools Who Dream)
from LA LA LAND

Music by Justin Hurwitz
Lyrics by Benj Pasek & Justin Paul

Registration 8
Rhythm: Waltz

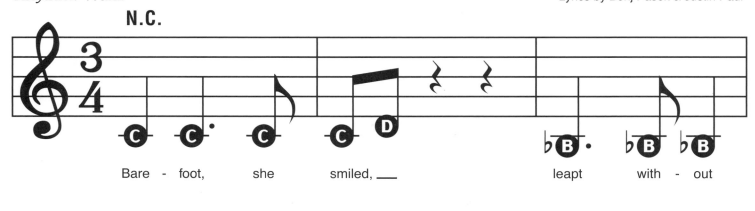

Bare - foot, she smiled, ___ leapt with - out

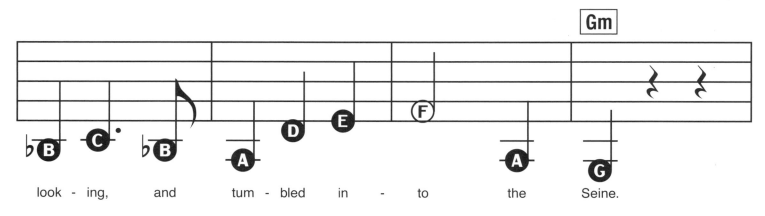

look - ing, and tum - bled in - to the Seine.

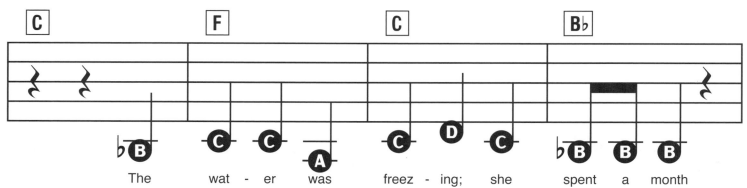

The wat - er was freez - ing; she spent a month

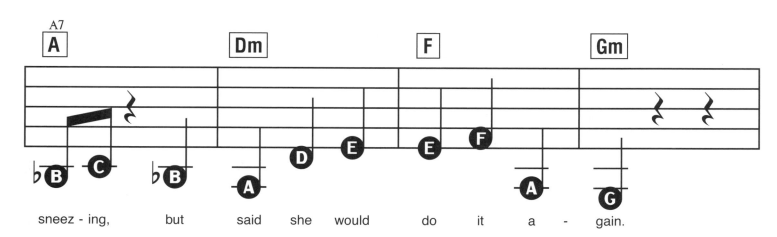

sneez - ing, but said she would do it a - gain.

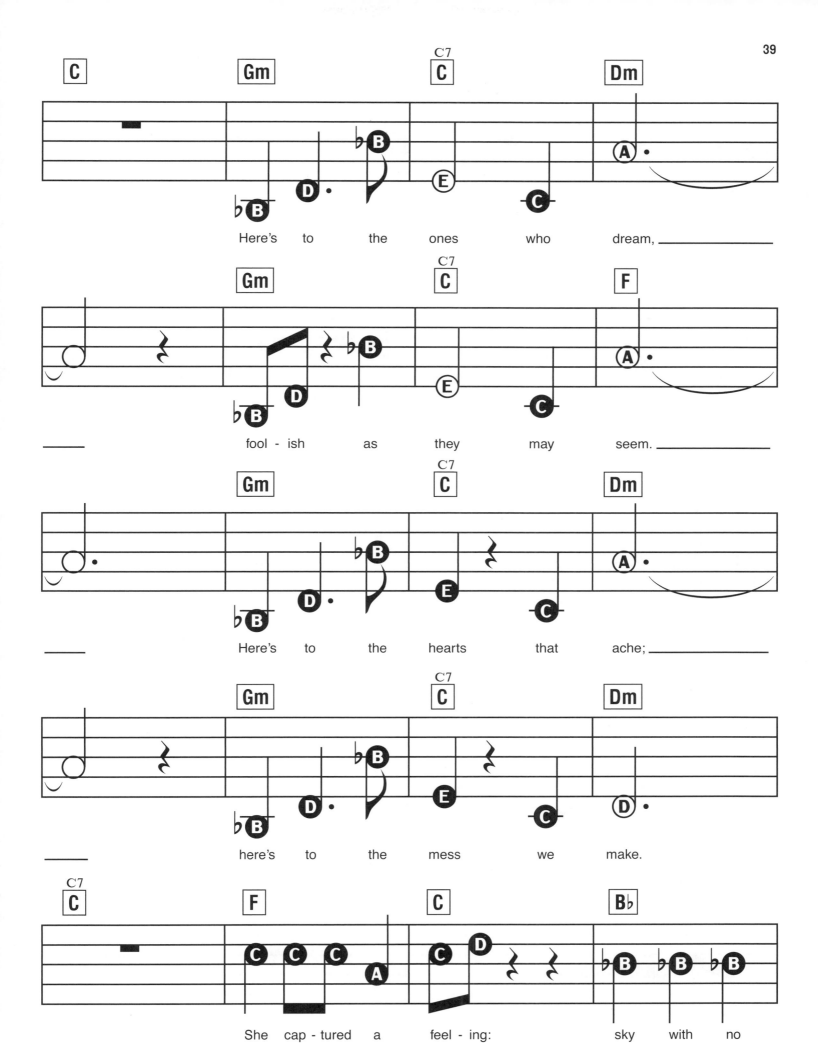

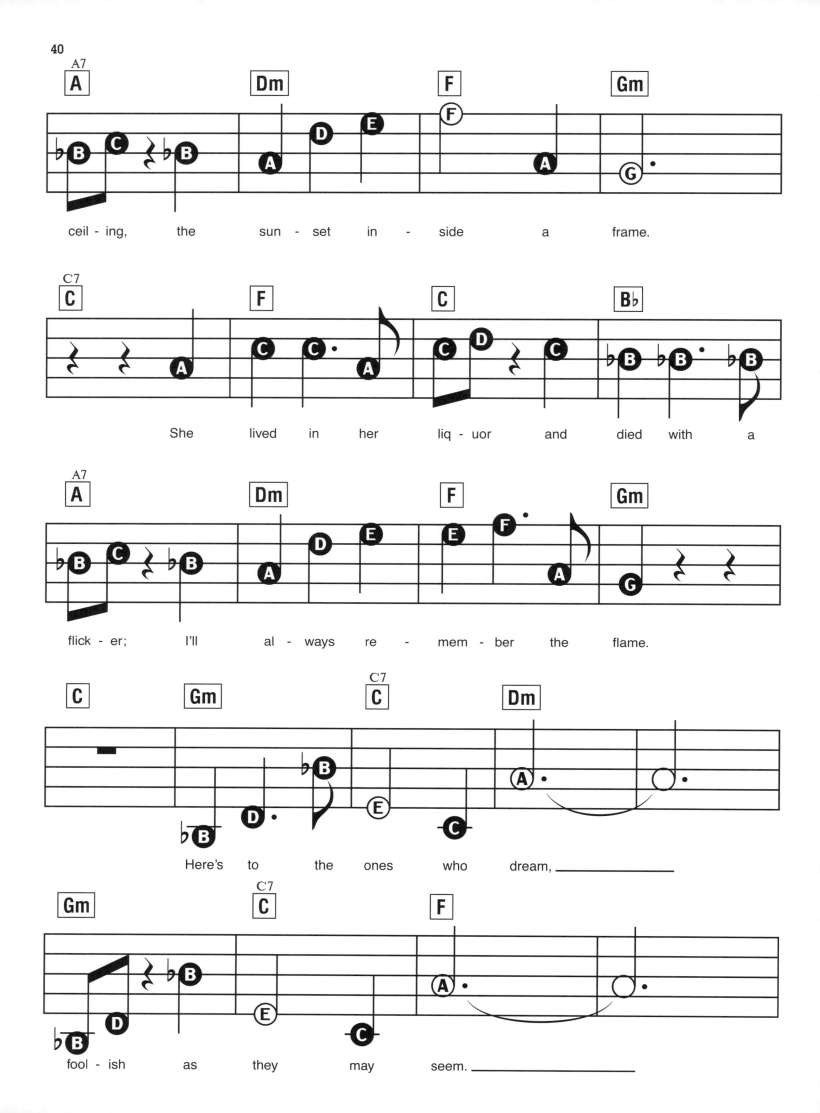

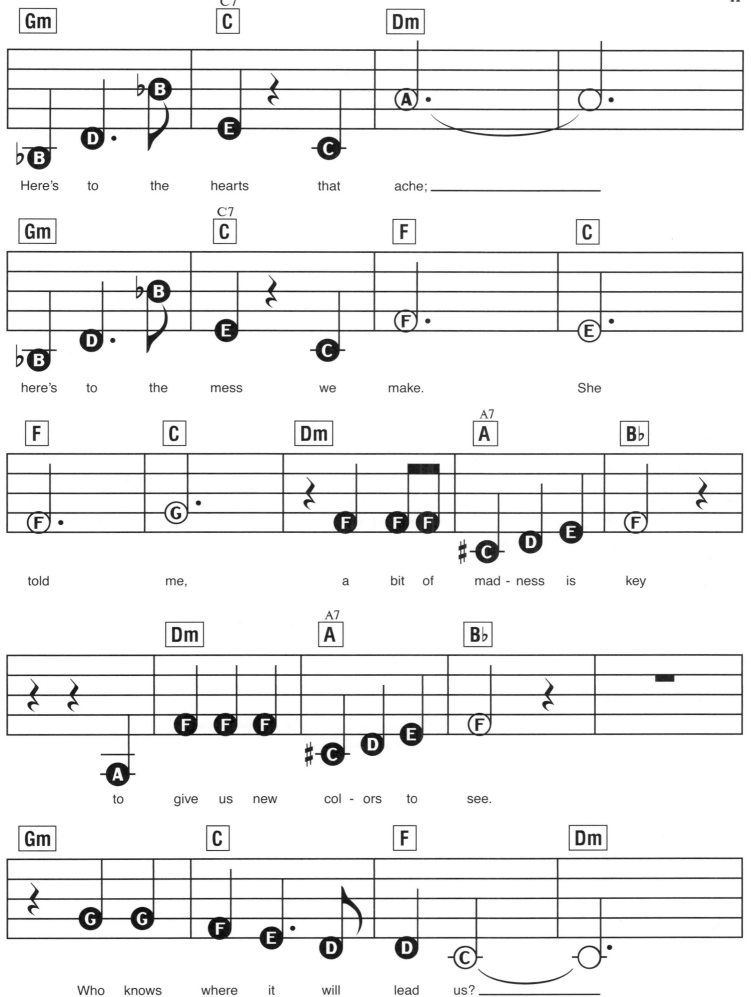

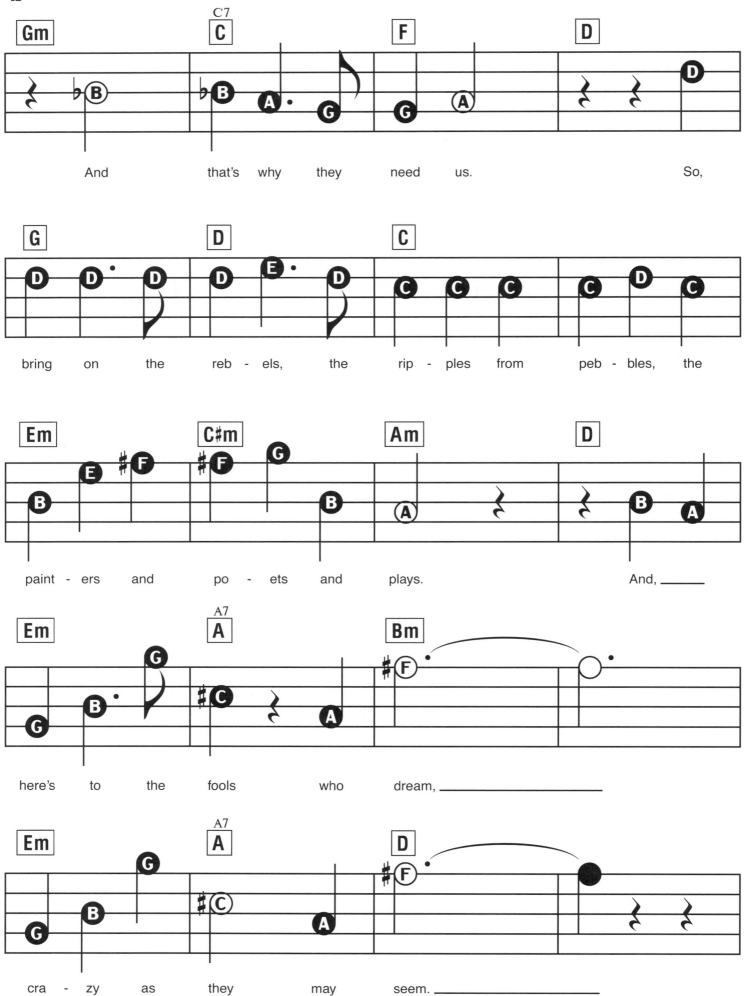

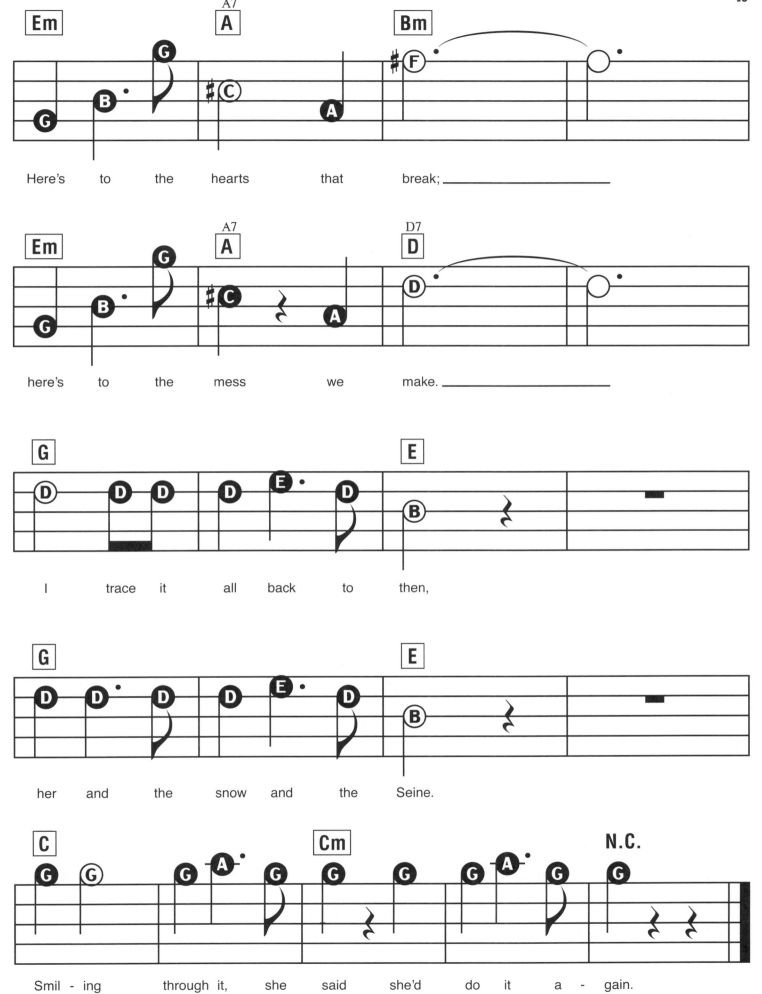

Here's to the hearts that break; _____

here's to the mess we make. _____

I trace it all back to then,

her and the snow and the Seine.

Smil - ing through it, she said she'd do it a - gain.

City of Stars
from LA LA LAND

Registration 8
Rhythm: Ballad

Music by Justin Hurwitz
Lyrics by Benj Pasek & Justin Paul

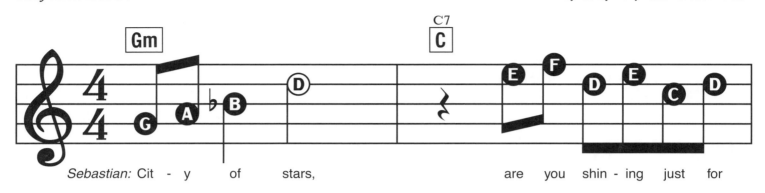

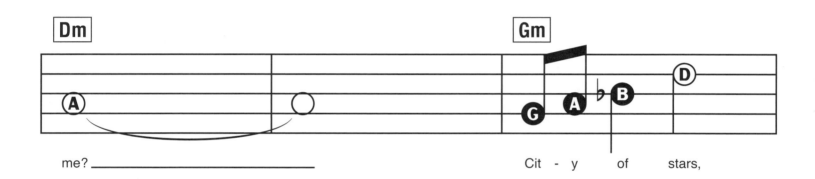

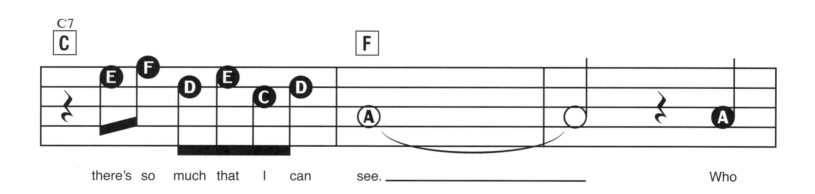

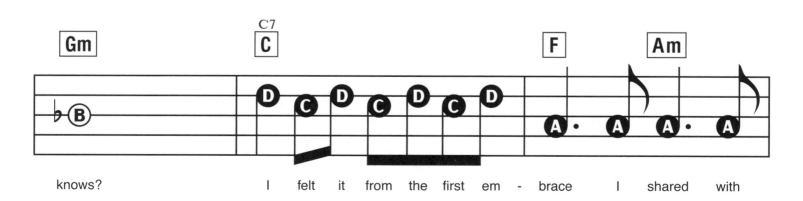

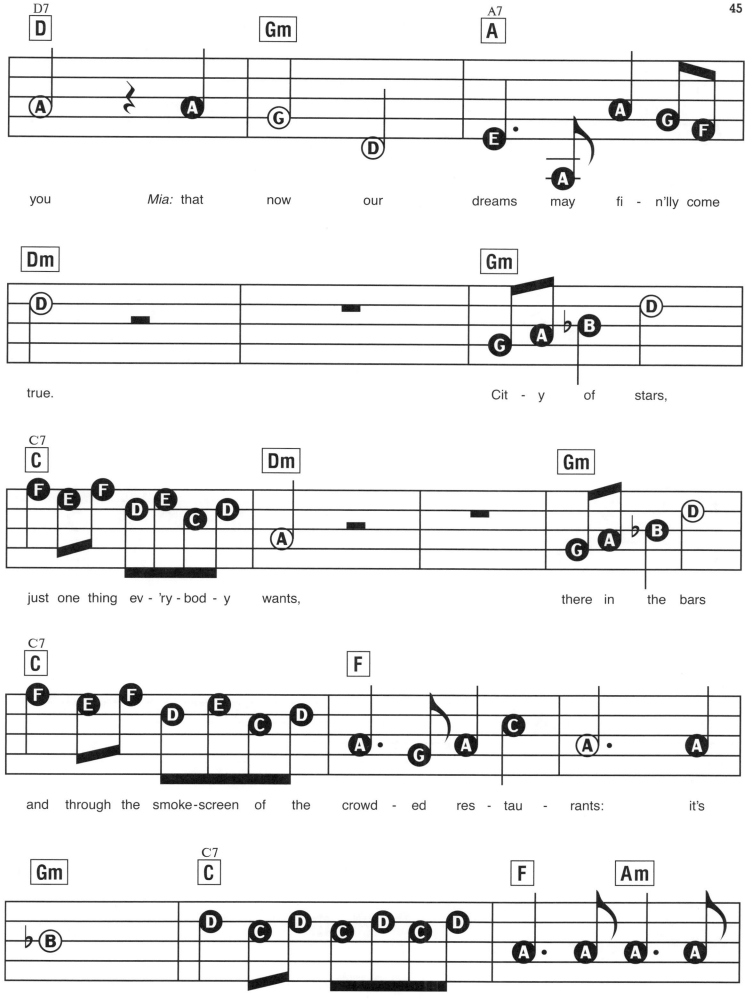

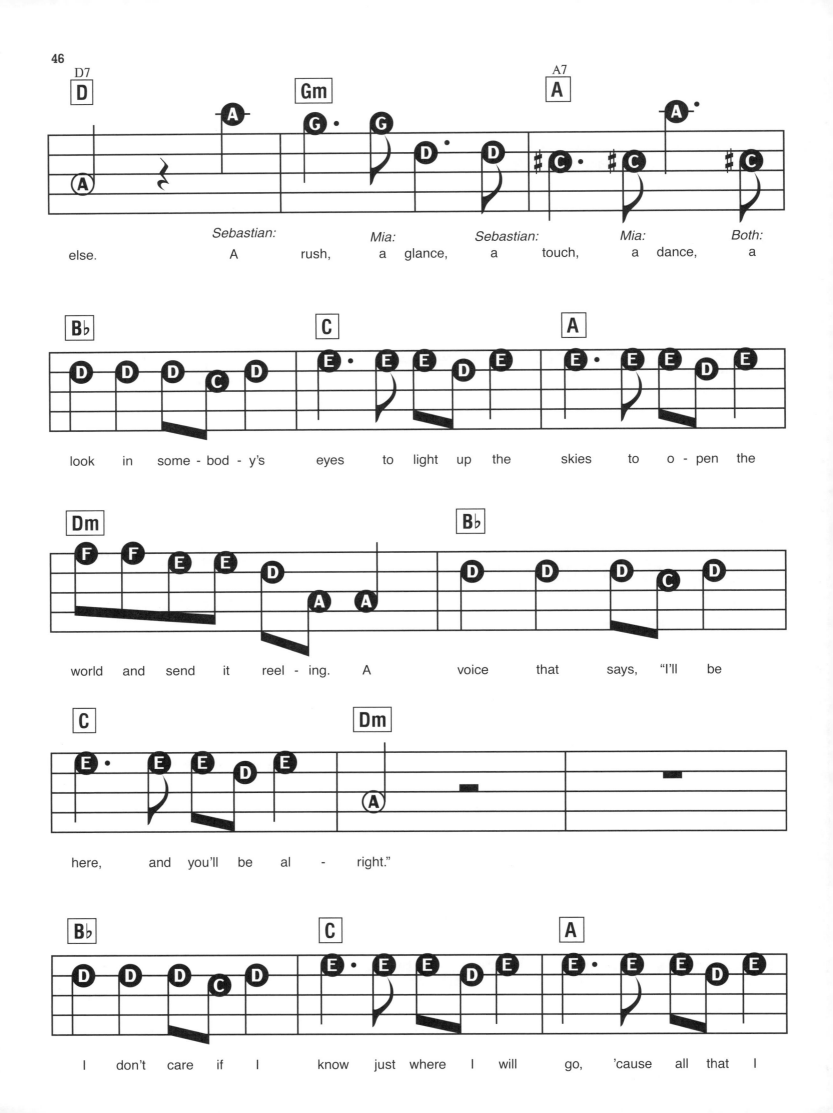

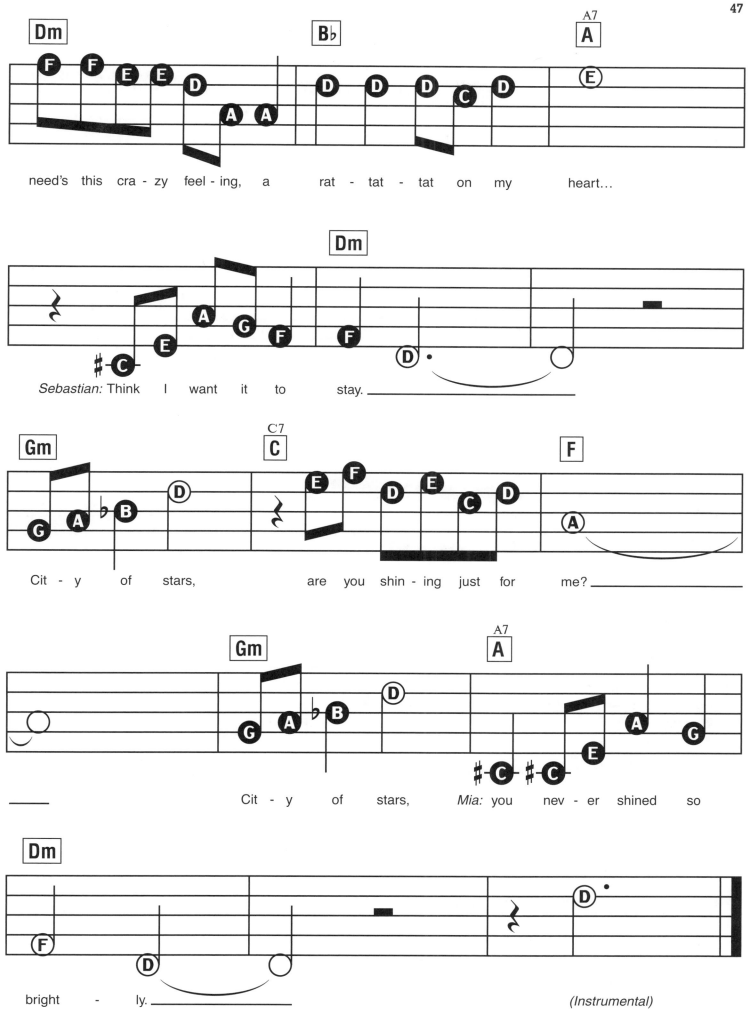

need's this cra - zy feel - ing, a   rat - tat - tat on my   heart...

Sebastian: Think I want it to   stay. _____

Cit - y of stars,   are you shin - ing just for   me? _____

_____ Cit - y of stars,   *Mia:* you nev - er shined so

bright - ly. _____   (Instrumental)

I Dreamed a Dream

from LES MISÉRABLES

Registration 1
Rhythm: Ballad

Music by Claude-Michel Schönberg
Lyrics by Alain Boublil, Jean-Marc Natel and Herbert Kretzmer

I dreamed a dream in time gone by
He slept a sum - mer by my side.

when hope was high and life worth liv - ing.
He filled my days with end - less won - der.

I dreamed that love would nev - er die.
He took my child - hood in his stride.

I dreamed that God would be for - giv - ing.

Then I was young and un - a - fraid.

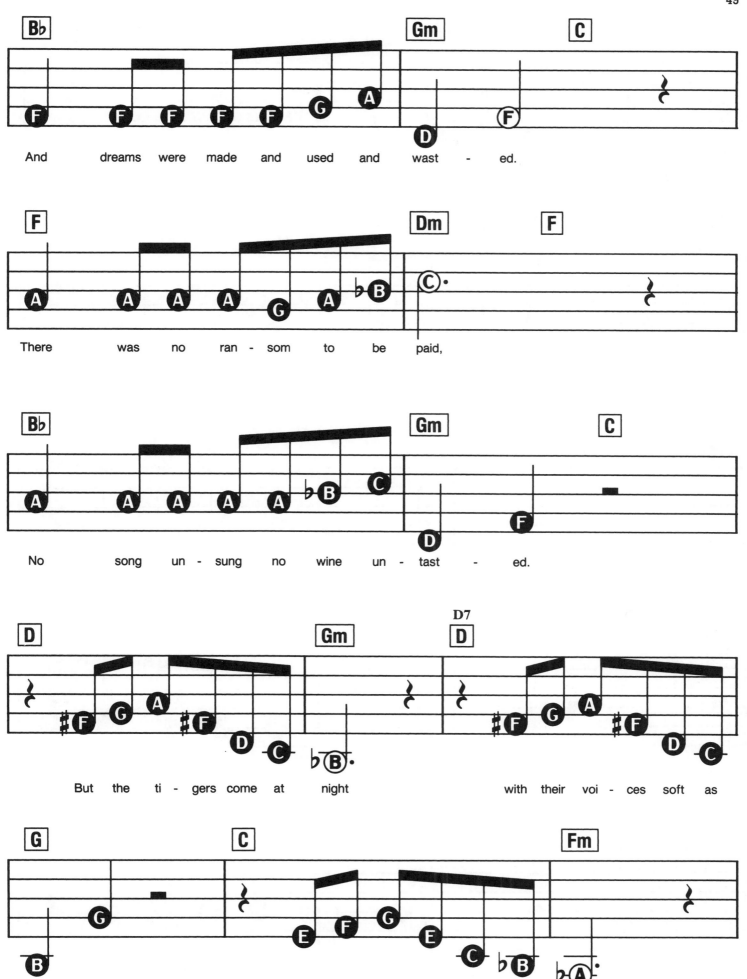

50

D.C. al Coda
(Return to beginning
Play to ⊕ and
skip to Coda)

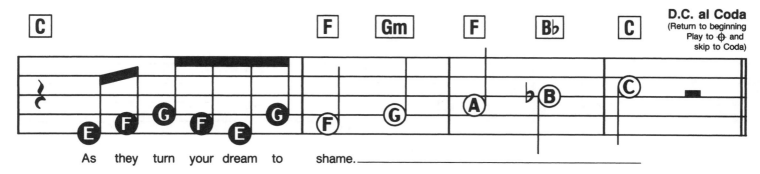

As they turn your dream to shame.

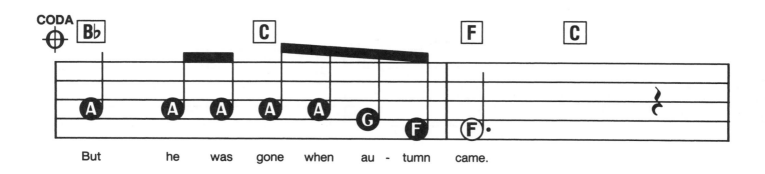

But he was gone when au - tumn came.

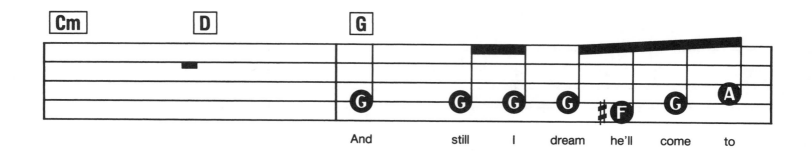

And still I dream he'll come to

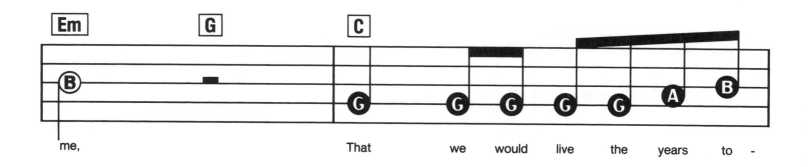

me, That we would live the years to -

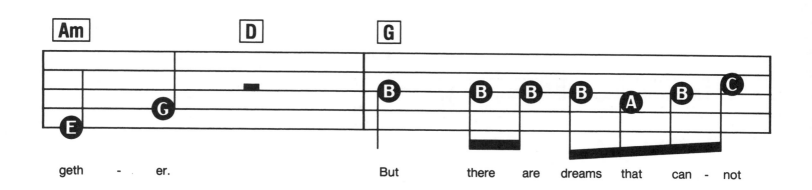

geth - er. But there are dreams that can - not

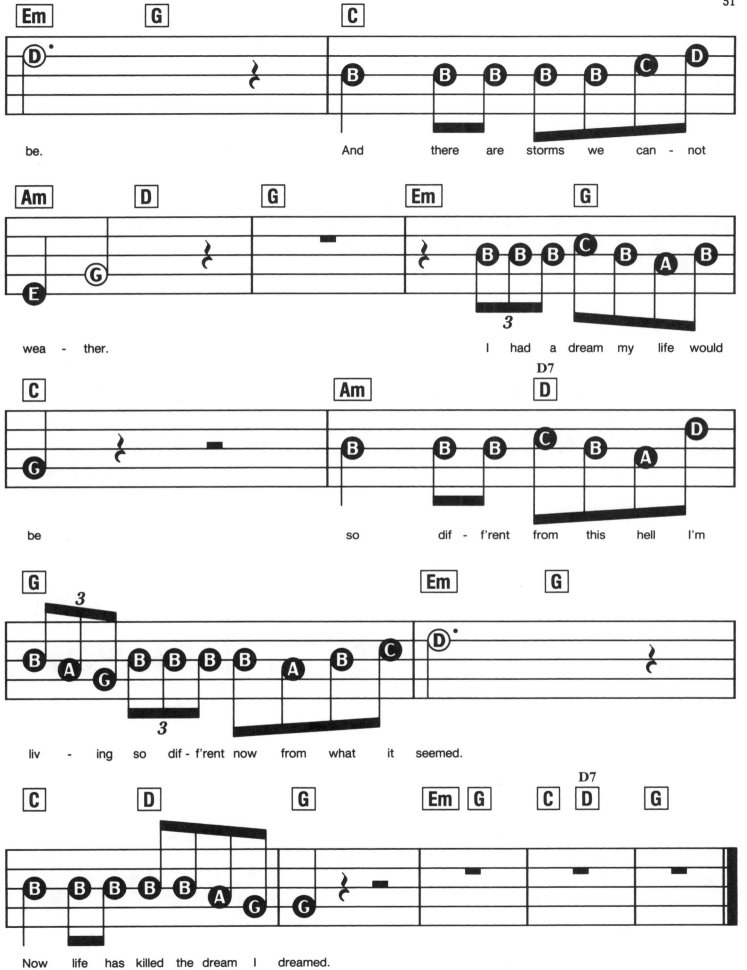

Fernando
featured in MAMMA MIA! HERE WE GO AGAIN

Registration 3
Rhythm: Latin

Words and Music by Benny Anderron,
Bjørn Ulvaeus and Stig Anderson

Can you hear the drums Fer - nan -do?   I re -mem -ber long a-

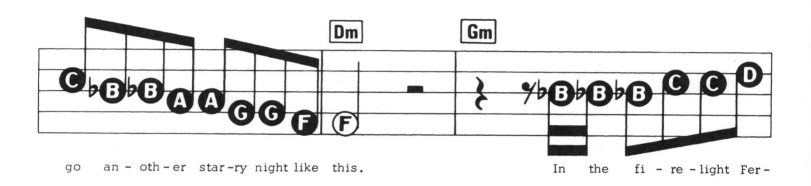

go an - oth -er star -ry night like this.   In the fi - re -light Fer-

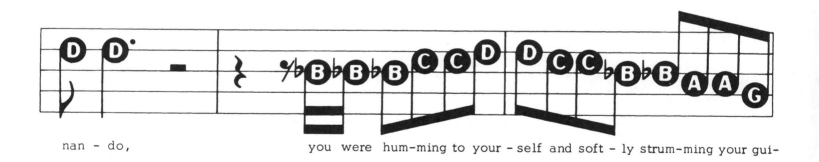

nan - do,   you were hum -ming to your -self and soft - ly strum -ming your gui-

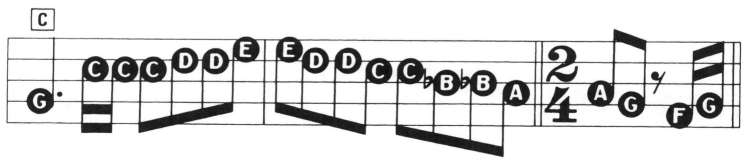

tar.   I could hear the dis -tant drums and sounds of bu -gle calls were   com -ing from a-

far.   They were clos- er   now Fer - nan - do.

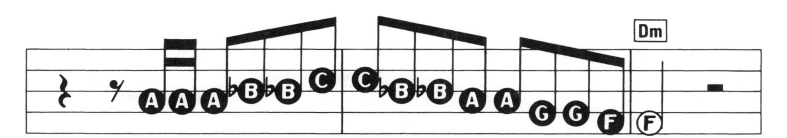

Ev -'ry ho - ur, ev -'ry min - ute seemed to last e - ter - nal - ly.

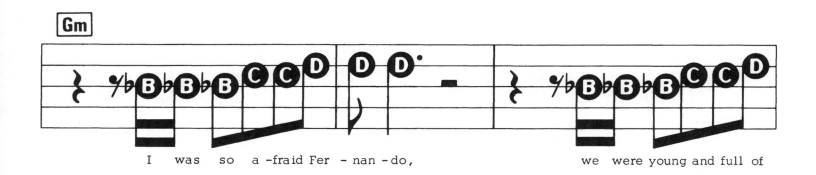

I was so a -fraid Fer - nan -do,   we were young and full of

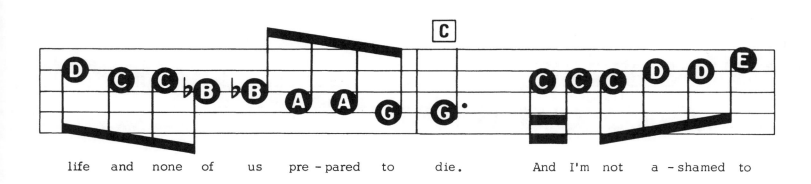

life and none of us pre - pared to die.   And I'm not a - shamed to

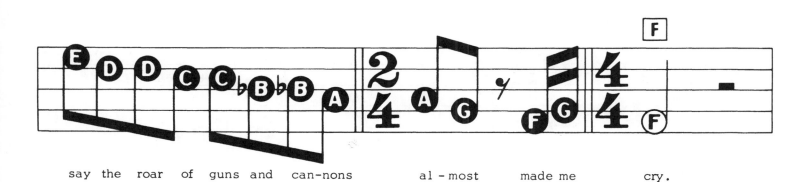

say the roar of guns and can -nons   al -most   made me   cry.

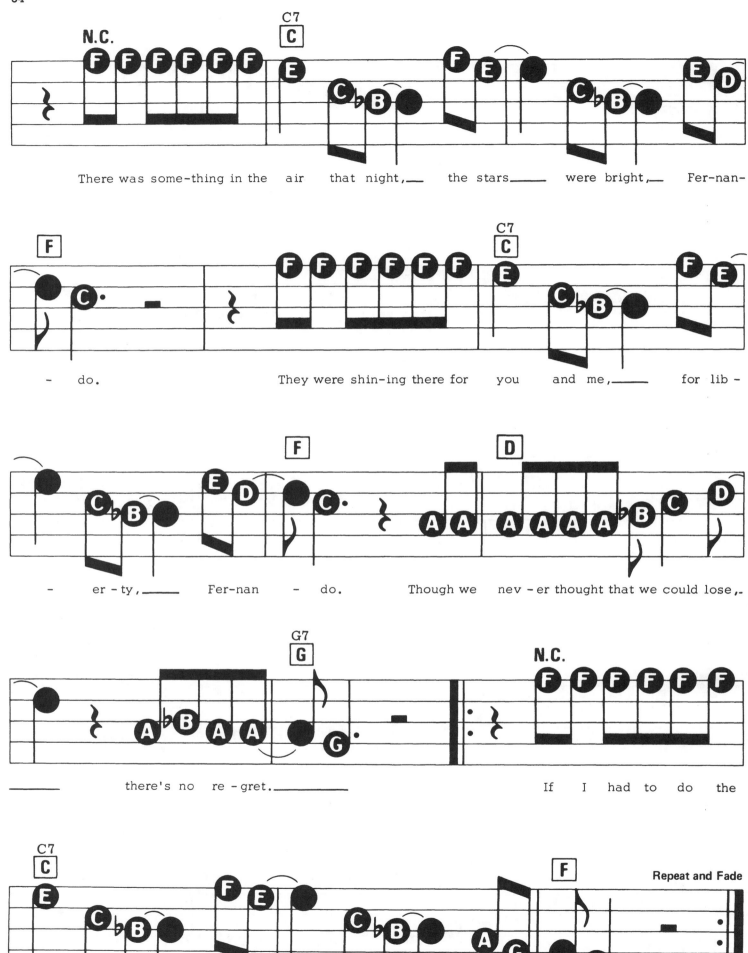

There was some-thing in the air that night,___ the stars___ were bright,___ Fer-nan-

- do. They were shin-ing there for you and me,___ for lib -

- er-ty,___ Fer-nan - do. Though we nev-er thought that we could lose,___

___ there's no re-gret.___ If I had to do the

same a-gain,___ I would___ my friend,___ Fer-nan - do.

Super Trouper
featured in MAMMA MIA! HERE WE GO AGAIN

Registration 1
Rhythm: Rock

Words and Music by Benny Andersson
and Bjørn Ulvaeus

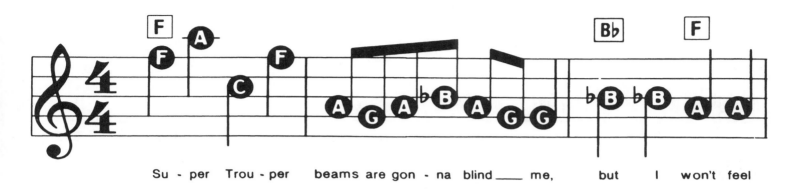

Su - per Trou - per beams are gon - na blind ___ me, but I won't feel

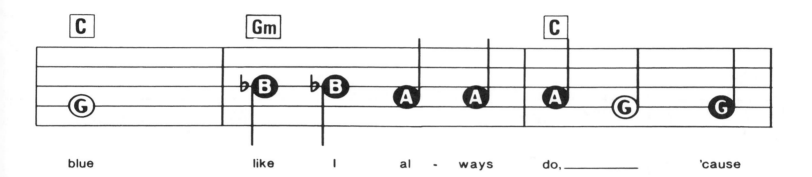

blue like I al - ways do, _____ 'cause

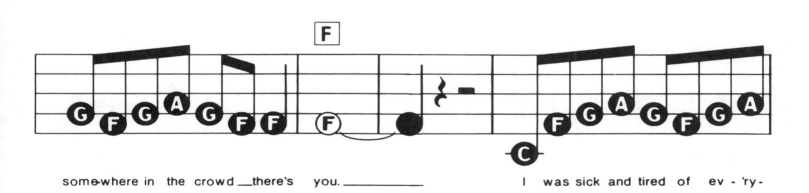

some-where in the crowd ___ there's you. _____ I was sick and tired of ev - 'ry-

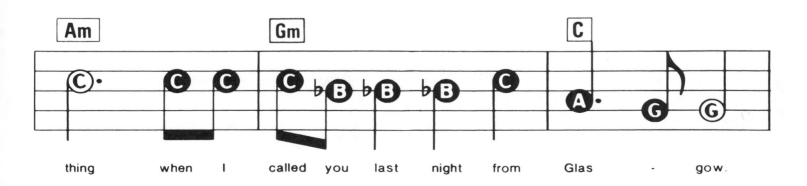

thing when I called you last night from Glas - gow.

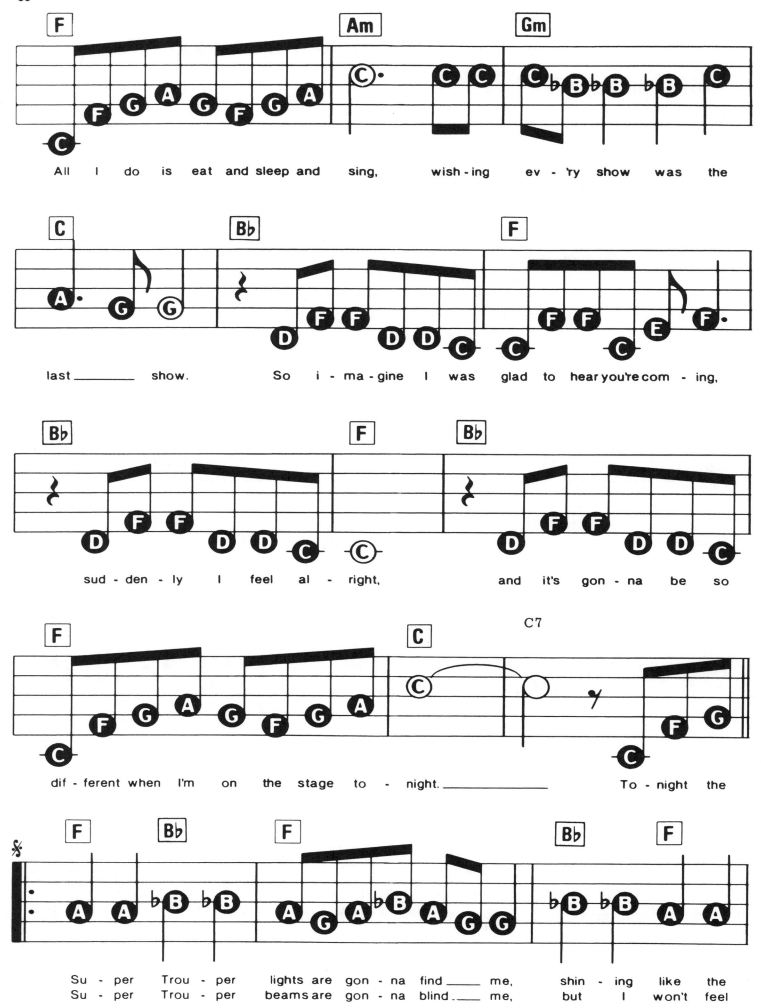

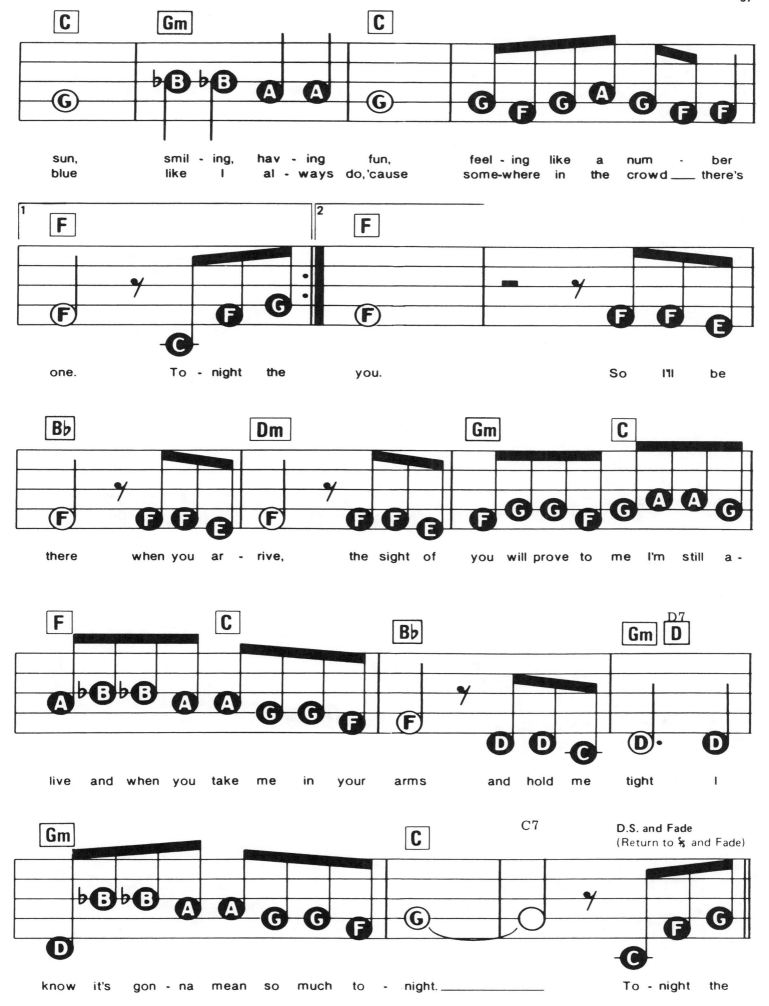

Mamma Mia
featured in MAMMA MIA! HERE WE GO AGAIN

Registration 3
Rhythm: Rock

Words and Music by Benny Andersson,
Björn Ulvaeus and Stig Anderson

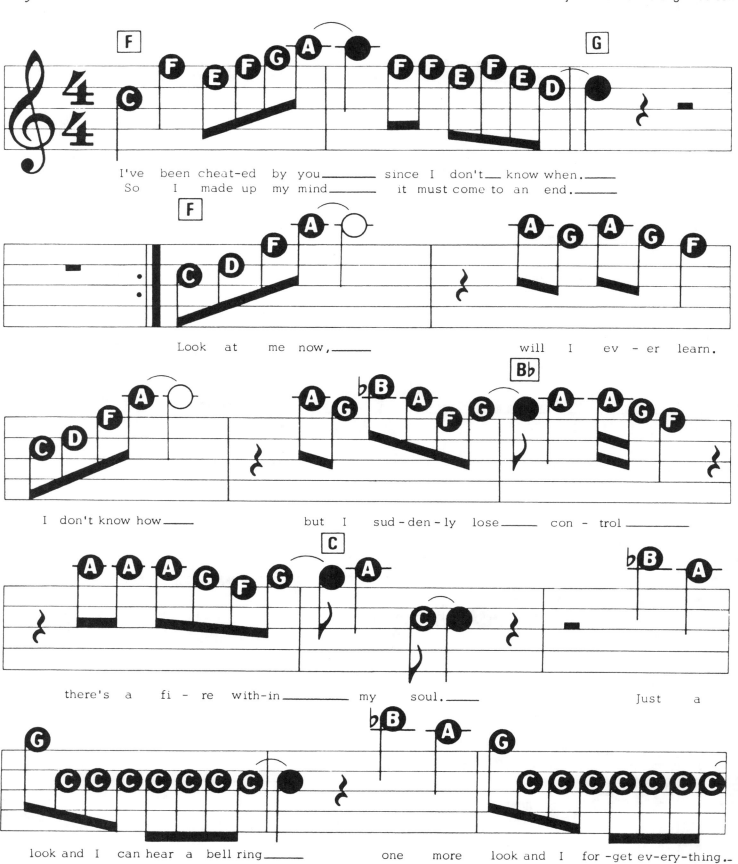

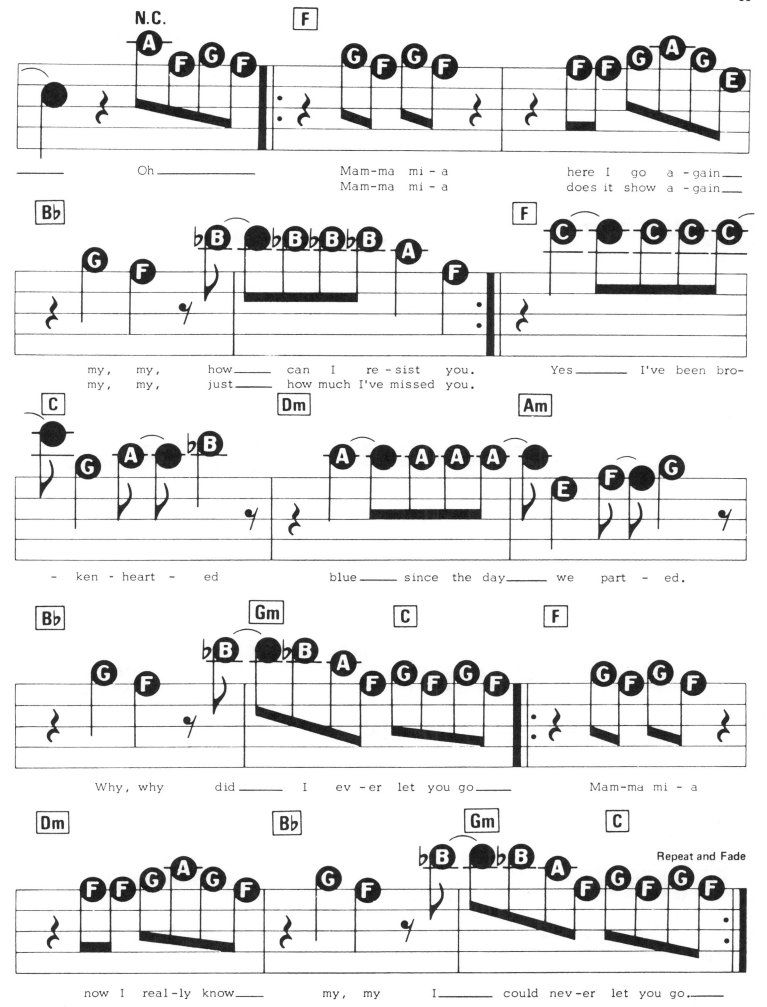

Always Remember Us This Way
from A STAR IS BORN

Registration 8
Rhythm: Ballad

Words and Music by Stefani Germanotta,
Hillary Lindsey, Natalie Hemby and Lori McKenna

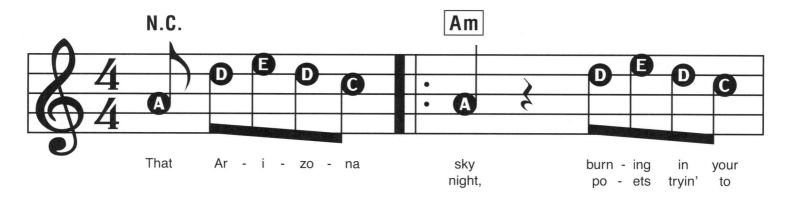

That Ar - i - zo - na sky burn - ing in your
night, po - ets tryin' to

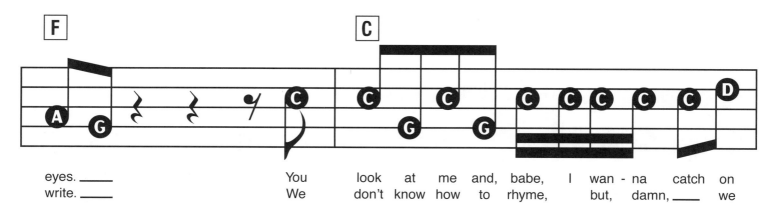

eyes. _____ You look at me and, babe, I wan - na catch on
write. _____ We don't know how to rhyme, but, damn, _____ we

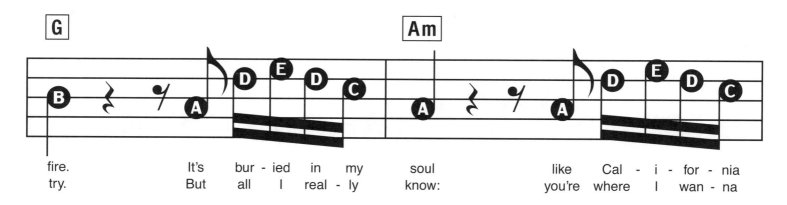

fire. It's bur - ied in my soul like Cal - i - for - nia
try. But all I real - ly know: you're where I wan - na

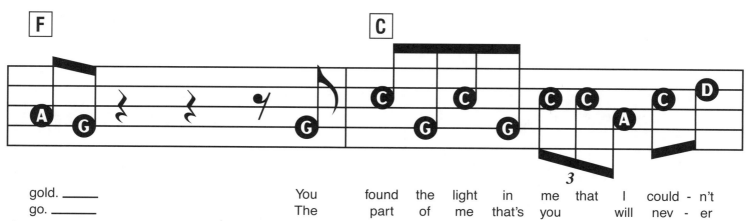

gold. _____ You found the light in me that I could - n't
go. _____ The part of me that's you will nev - er

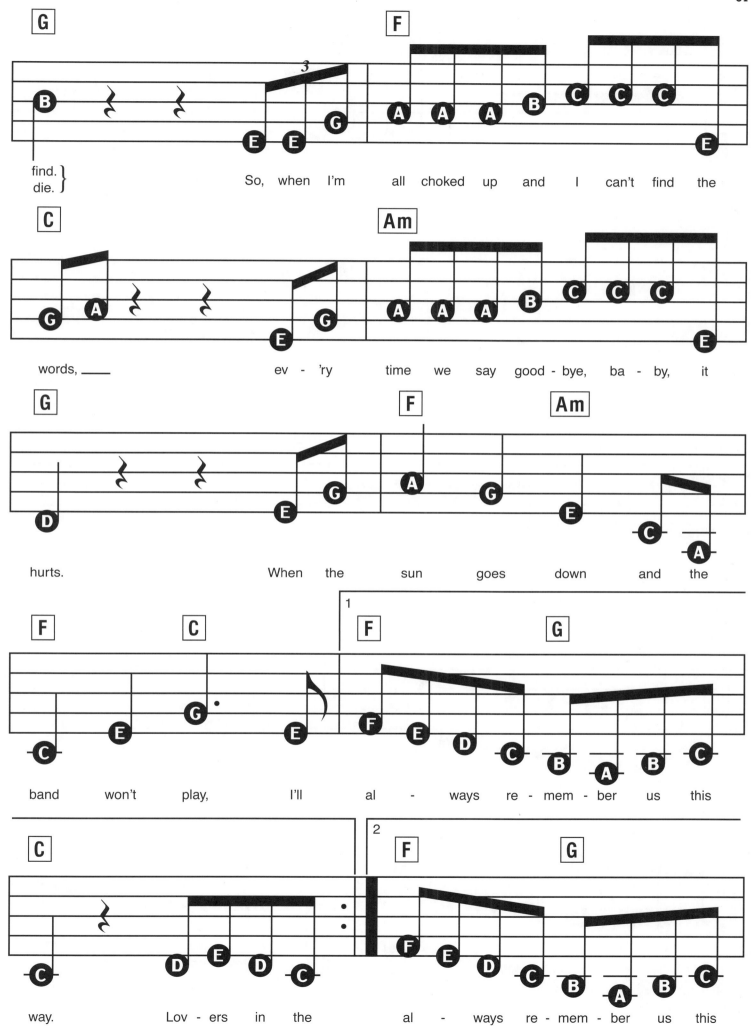

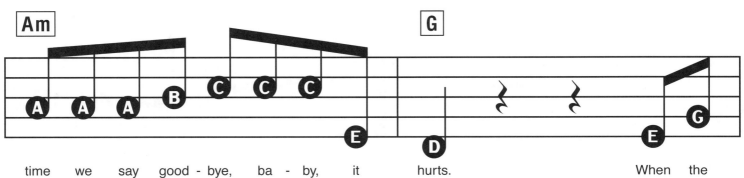

B♭

C A

C

way, oh, yeah.

F

♭E D C A C C A C C

♭E D C C

I don't wan-na be just a mem-o-ry, ba-by, yeah.

C

♭E D C ♭E D C C C

Oo, _____ oo, _____ oo, oo.

B♭

♭E D C ♭E D C C C

Oo, _____ oo, _____ oo, oo.

F

♭E D C ♭E D C C C

Oo, _____ oo, _____ oo, oo, oo.

G

D G A

When I'm

F

A A A B C C ♭E D C

all choked up and I can't find ____ the words, _____

C

C G A G E G

ev-'ry

Am

A A A B C C C E D

time we say good-bye, ba-by, it hurts.

G

E G

When the

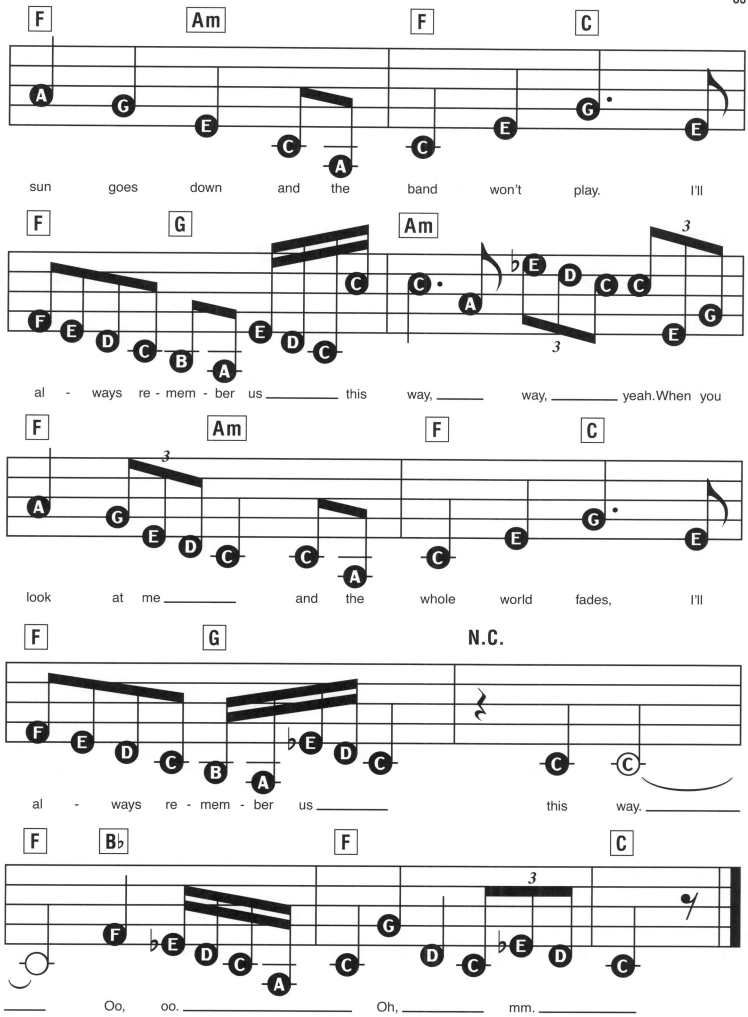

I'll Never Love Again
from A STAR IS BORN

Registration 8
Rhythm: Ballad or 8-Beat

Words and Music by Stefani Germanotta,
Aaron Raitiere, Hillary Lindsey and Natalie Hemby

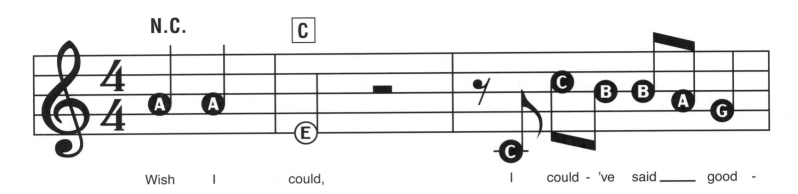

Wish I could, I could-'ve said ____ good-

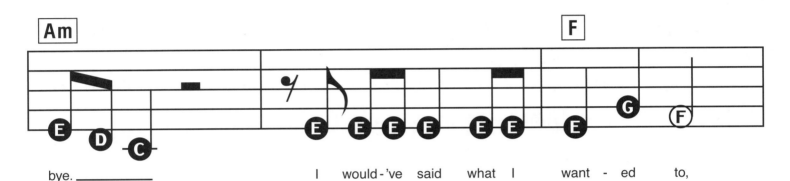

bye. ____ I would-'ve said what I want-ed to,

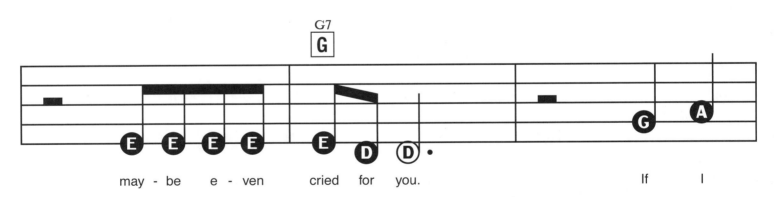

may-be e-ven cried for you. If I

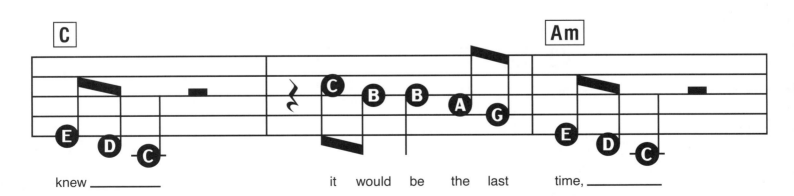

knew ____ it would be the last time, ____

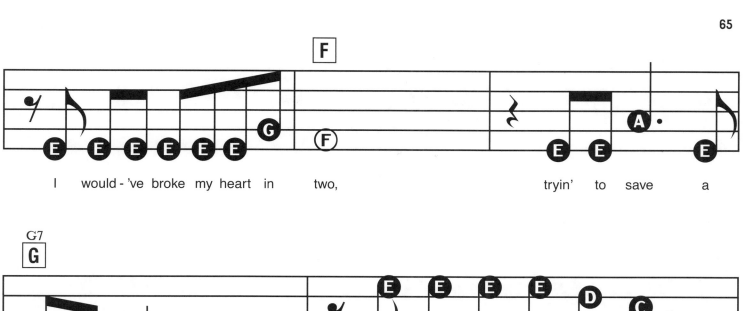

I would-'ve broke my heart in two, tryin' to save a

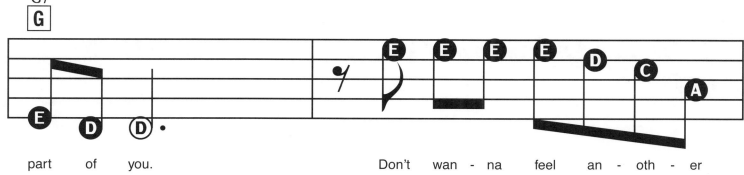

part of you. Don't wan - na feel an - oth - er

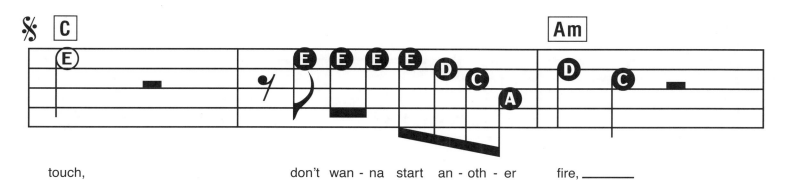

touch, don't wan - na start an - oth - er fire, _____

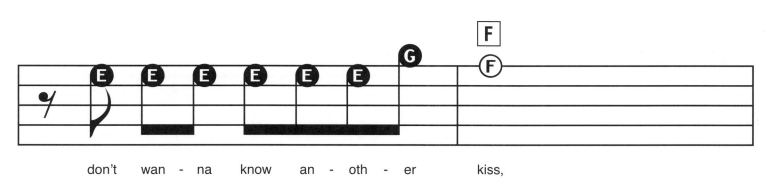

don't wan - na know an - oth - er kiss,

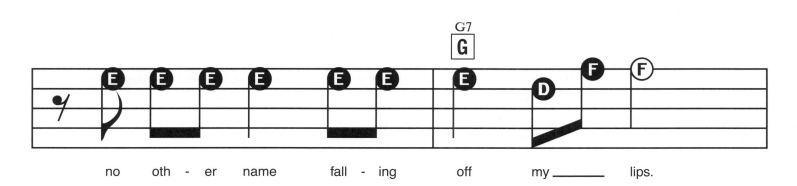

no oth - er name fall - ing off my _____ lips.

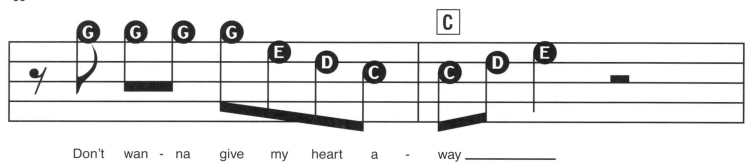

Don't wan - na give my heart a - way _____

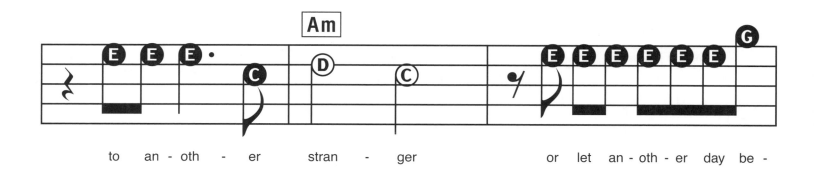

to an - oth - er stran - ger   or let an - oth - er day be -

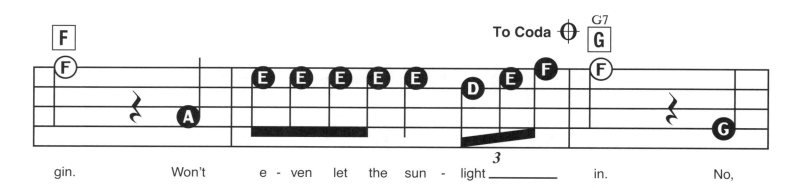

gin.   Won't e - ven let the sun - light _____ in.   No,

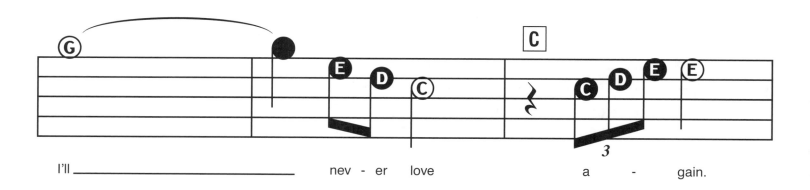

I'll _____   nev - er love   a - gain.

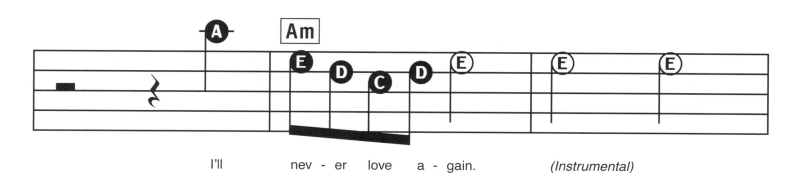

I'll   nev - er love a - gain.   (Instrumental)

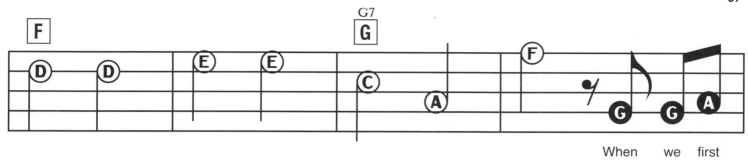

When we first

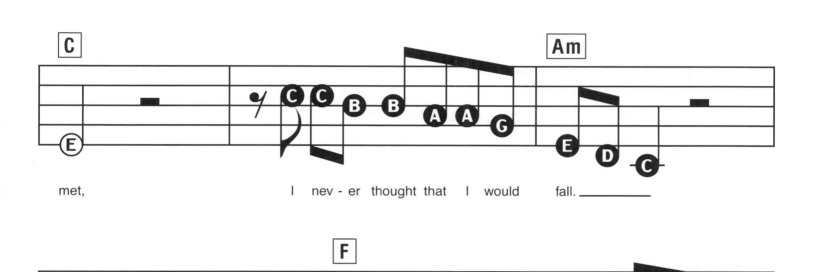

met, I nev - er thought that I would fall. _____

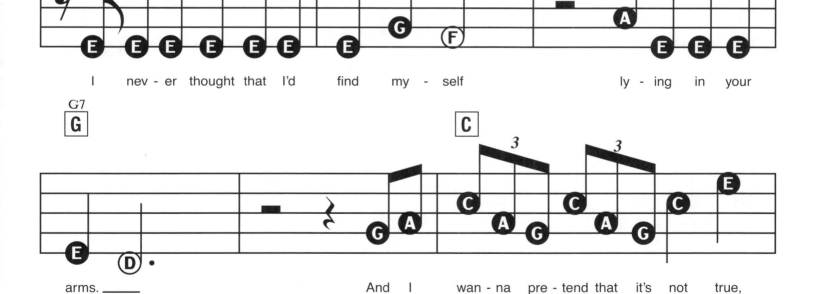

I nev - er thought that I'd find my - self ly - ing in your

arms. ____ And I wan - na pre - tend that it's not true,

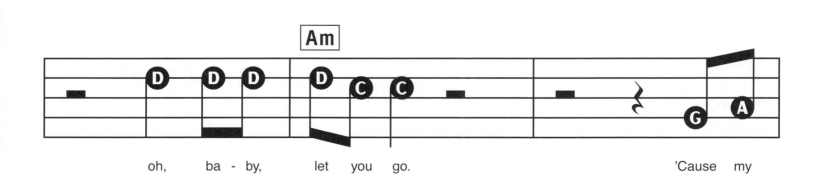

oh, ba - by, let you go. 'Cause my

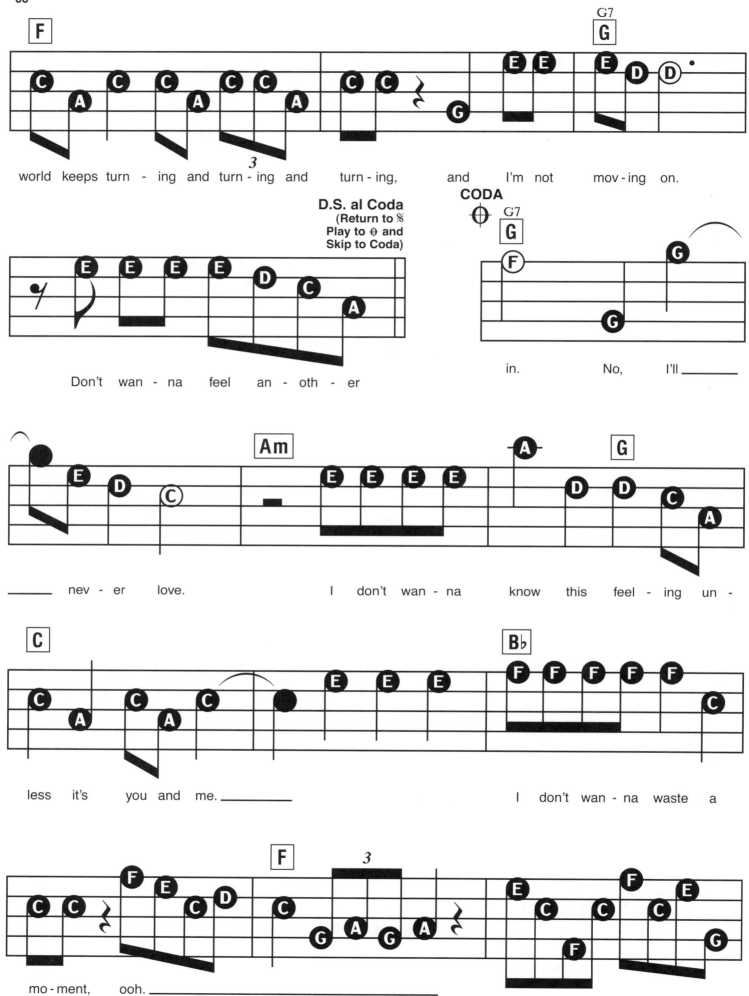

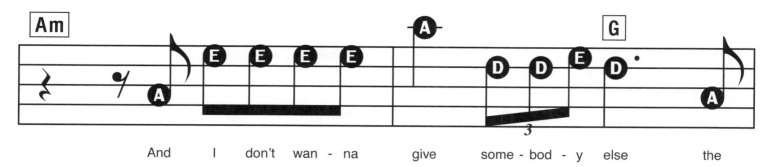

And I don't wan - na give some - bod - y else the

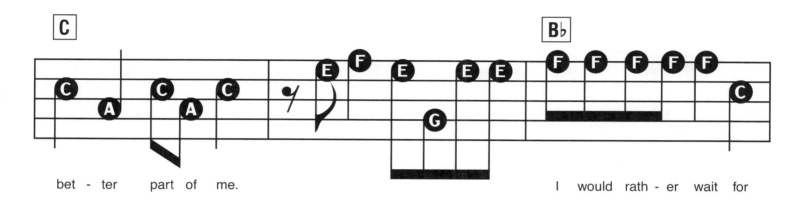

bet - ter part of me. I would rath - er wait for

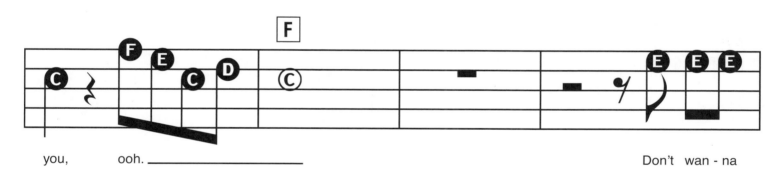

you, ooh. _____ Don't wan - na

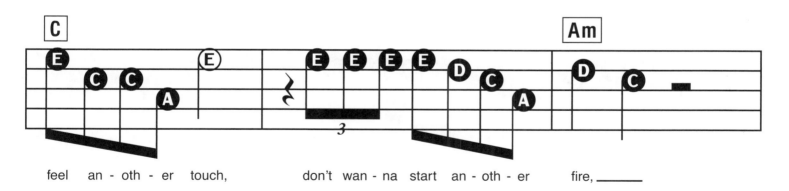

feel an - oth - er touch, don't wan - na start an - oth - er fire, _____

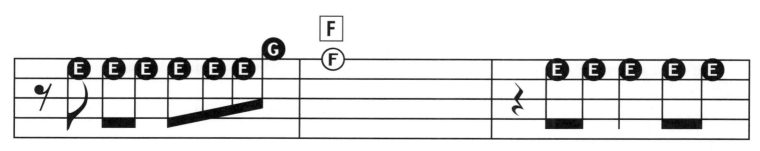

don't wan - na know an - oth - er kiss, ba - by, un - less they

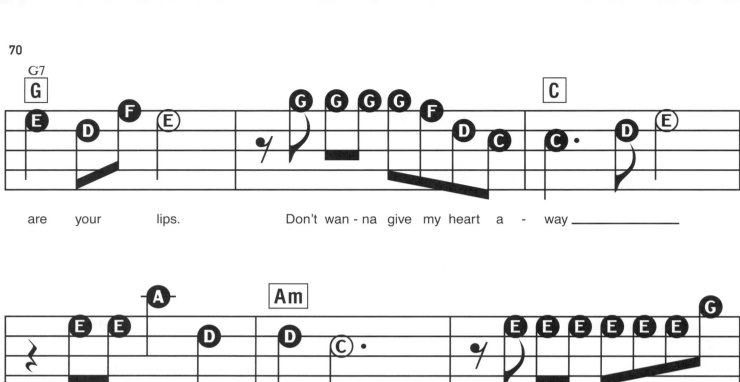

are your lips. Don't wan-na give my heart a - way _____

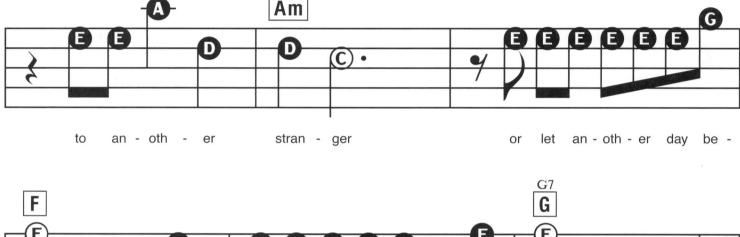

to an - oth - er stran - ger   or let an - oth - er day be -

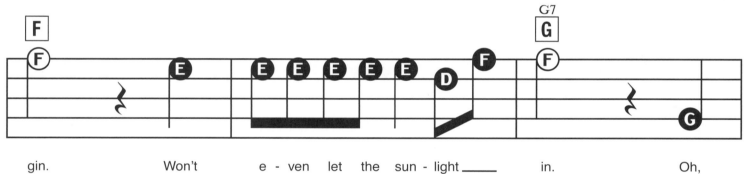

gin.   Won't   e - ven let the sun - light _____ in.   Oh,

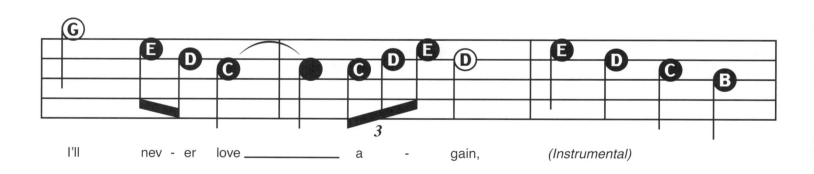

I'll   nev - er love _____ a - gain,   (Instrumental)

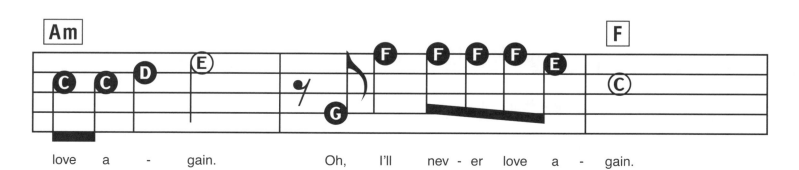

love a - gain.   Oh, I'll   nev - er love a - gain.

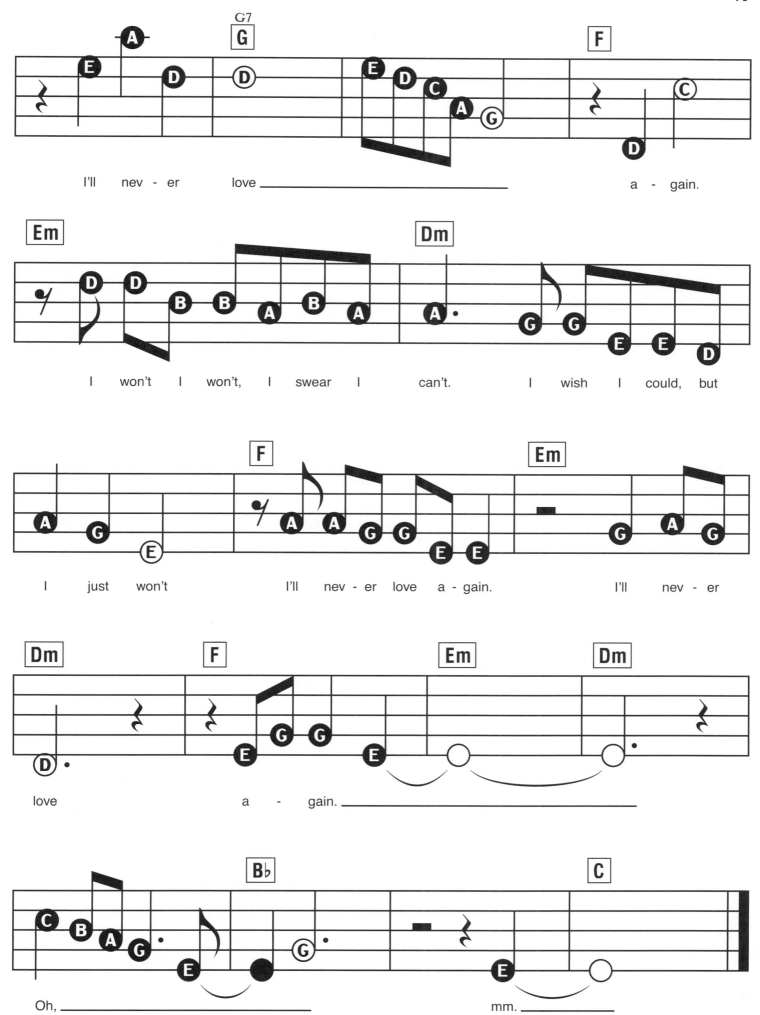

Is That Alright?
from A STAR IS BORN

Words and Music by Stefani Germanotta,
Aaron Raitiere, Nick Monson, Lukas Nelson,
Mark Nilan Jr. and Paul Blair

Registration 8
Rhythm: Ballad

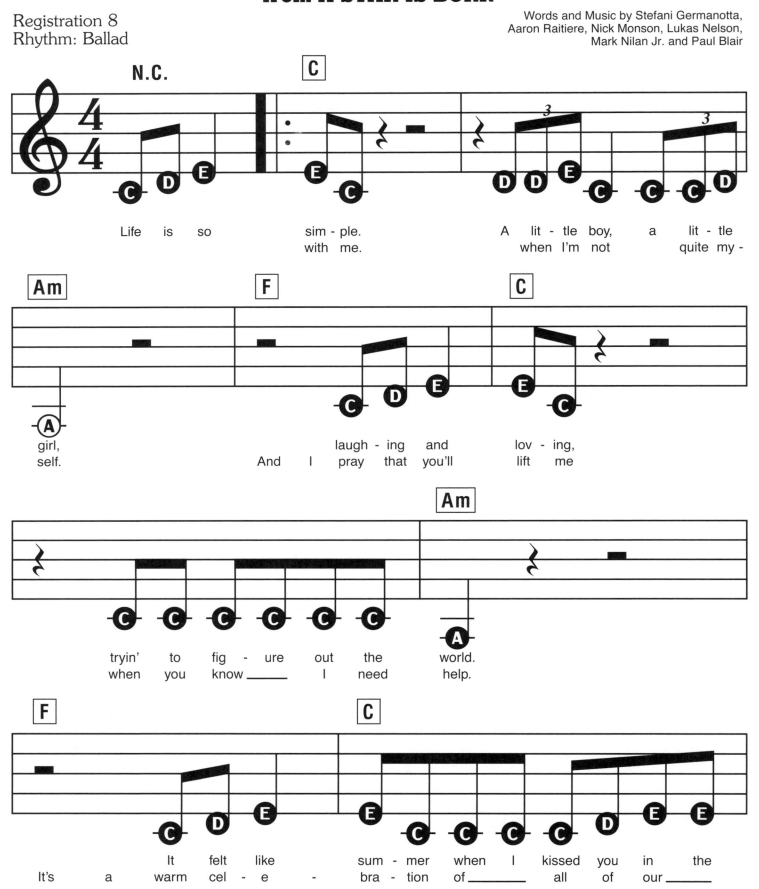

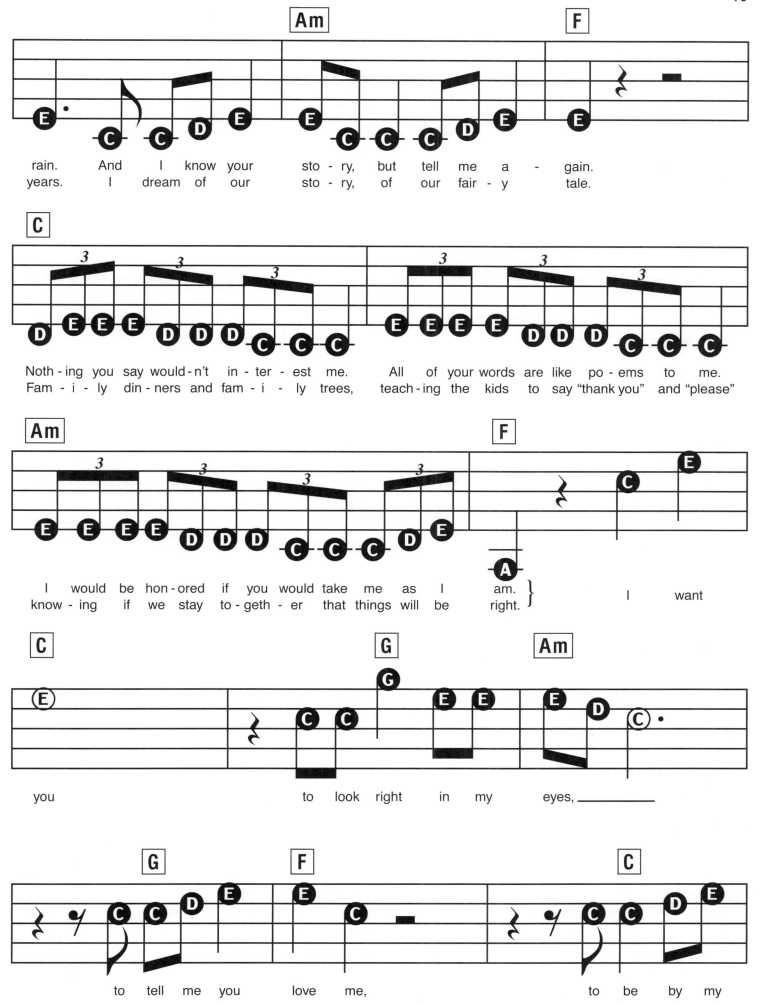

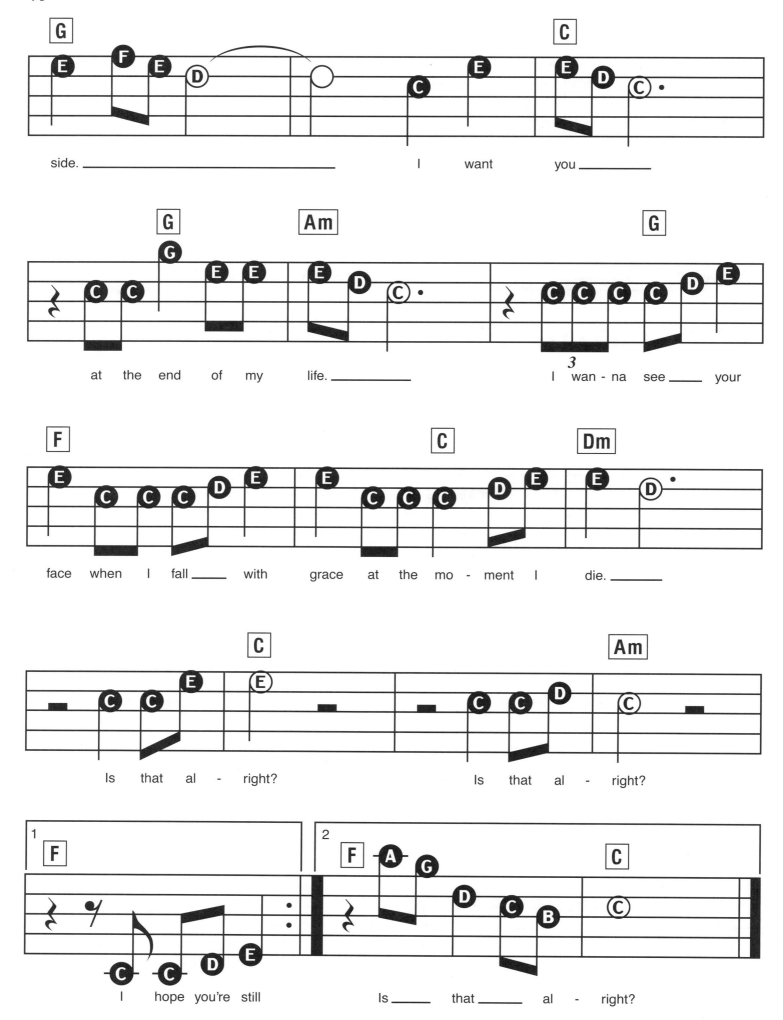

Music to My Eyes
from A STAR IS BORN

Registration 4
Rhythm: Country Rock or Ballad

Words and Music by Stefani Germanotta
and Lukas Nelson

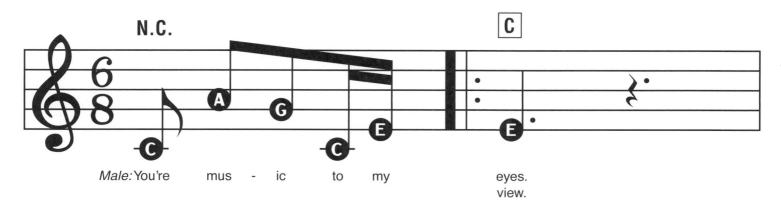

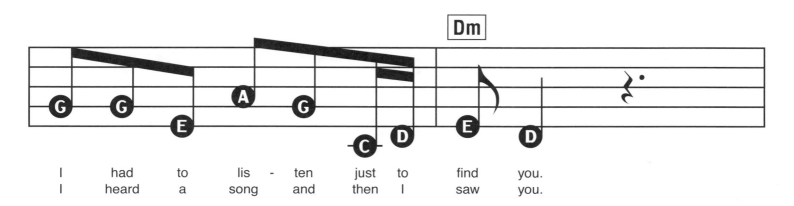

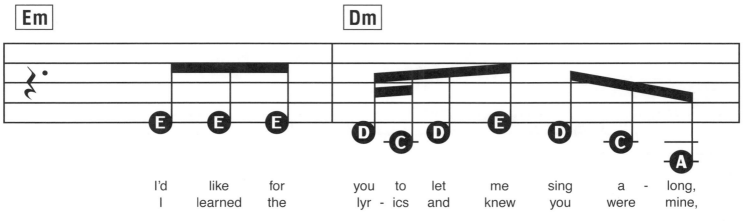

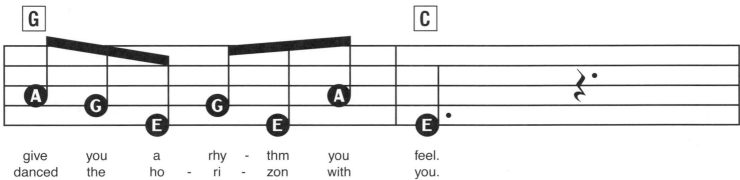

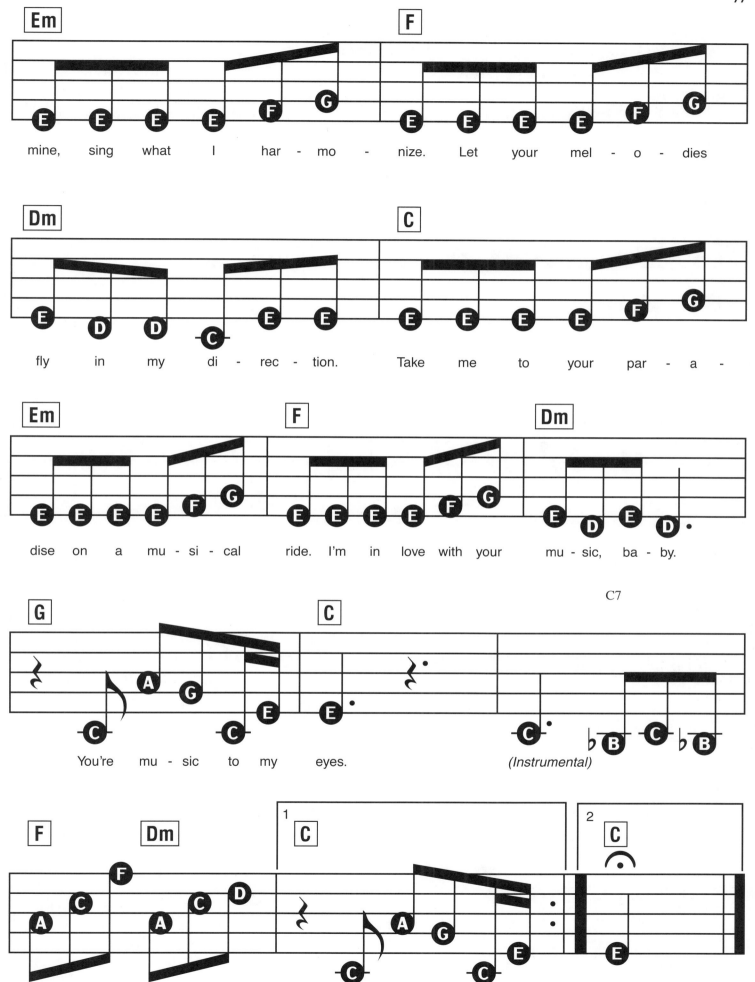

mine, sing what I har - mo - nize. Let your mel - o - dies
fly in my di - rec - tion. Take me to your par - a -
dise on a mu - si - cal ride. I'm in love with your mu - sic, ba - by.
You're mu - sic to my eyes. *(Instrumental)*
Female: Your voice is quite a

Look What I Found
from A STAR IS BORN

Registration 8
Rhythm: Rock or R&B

Words and Music by Stefani Germanotta,
Aaron Raitiere, Nick Monson, Lukas Nelson,
Mark Nilan Jr. and Paul Blair

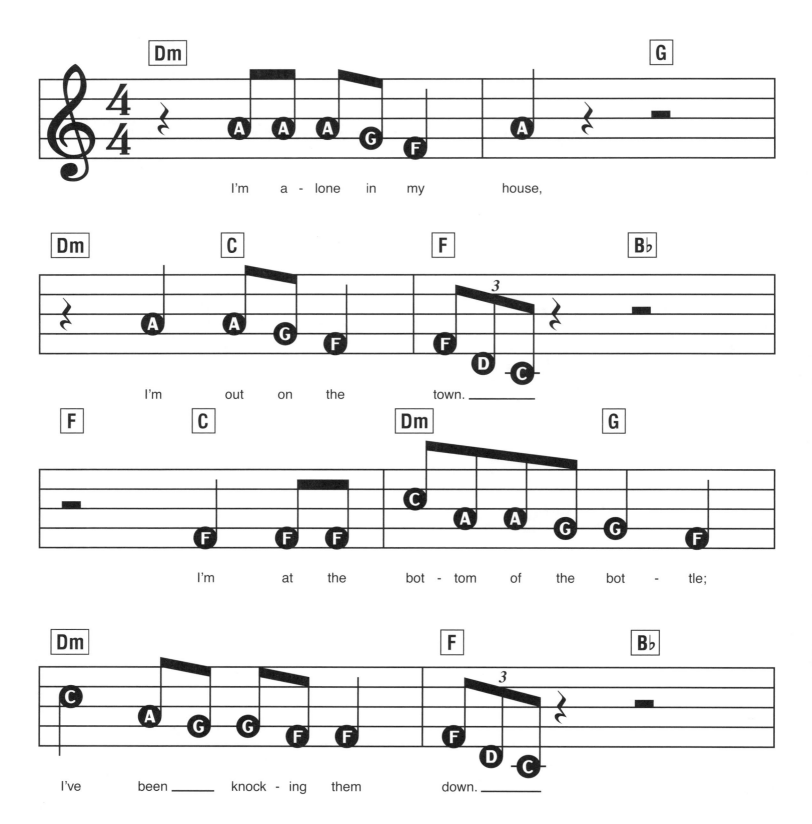

I'm a - lone in my house,

I'm out on the town. _____

I'm at the bot - tom of the bot - tle;

I've been _____ knock - ing them down. _____

B♭

G F D A G F D

_____ just lay - ing on the ground.

Dm   **G**

F

Dm   **G**   **Dm**   **C**

A A A G F   A   A A A G F

Un - der the fog - gy day,   I'm look - ing for a

F   **B♭**   **F**   **C**   **Dm**   **G**

F D C   A A G F   C C

_3_

light. _____   And my on - ly friend _____

Dm   **C**   **F**   **B♭**   **F**   A7 **A**

A A G F   F G A   F F F

is work - ing to - night. _____   I can't get

Dm   F7 **F**

C A A G G F F   C A A G G F F

my - self out of bed, hear these voic - es in my head like a

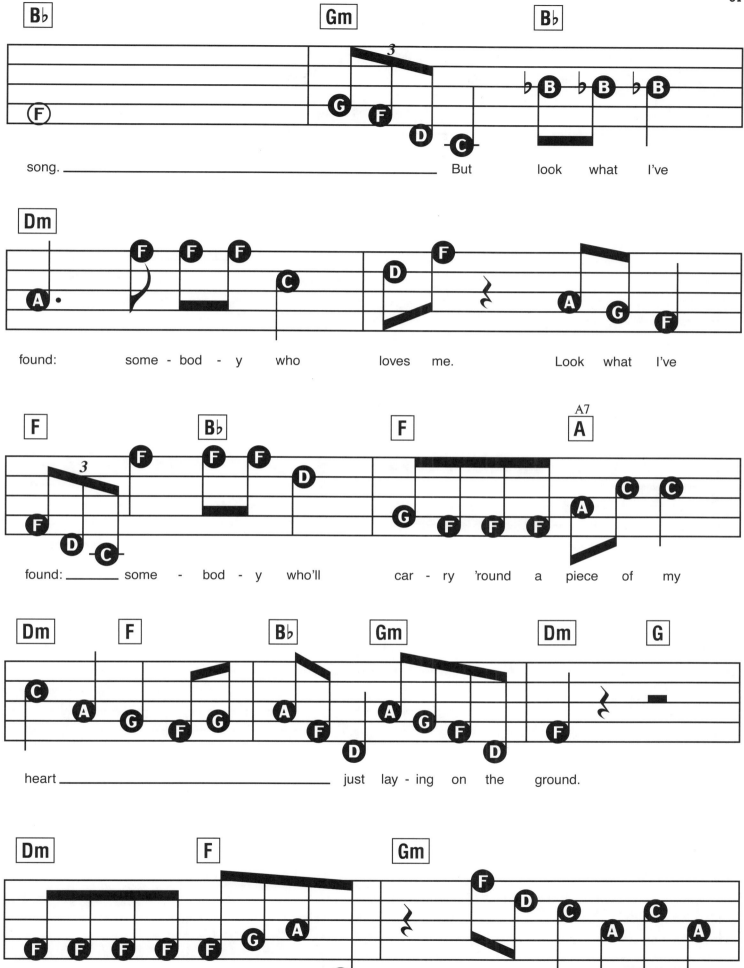

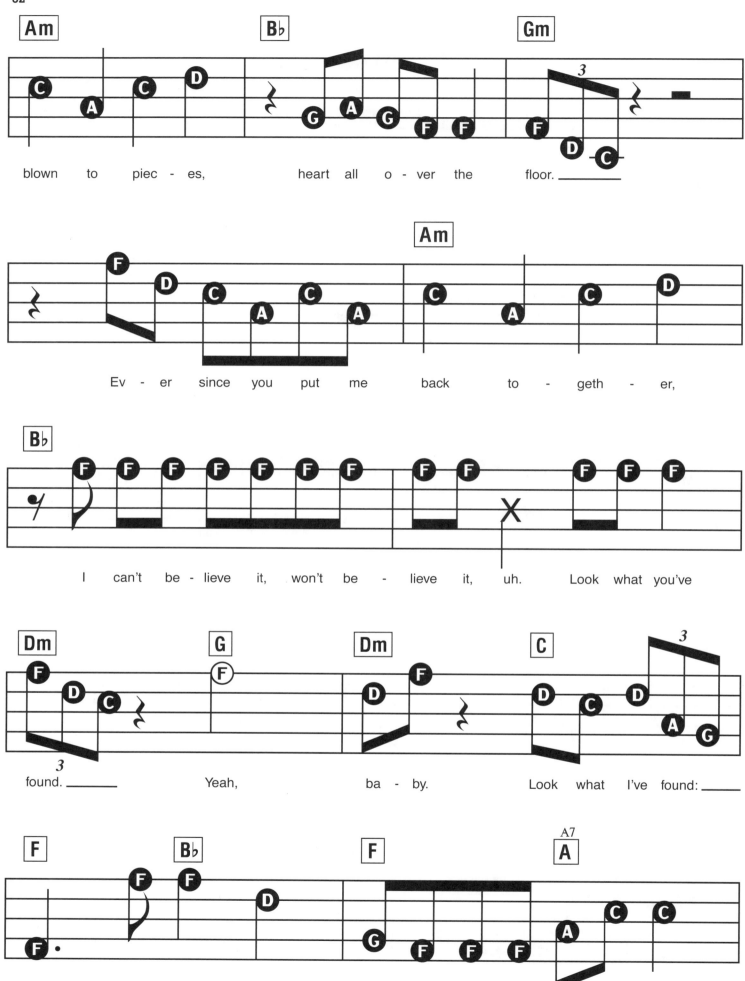

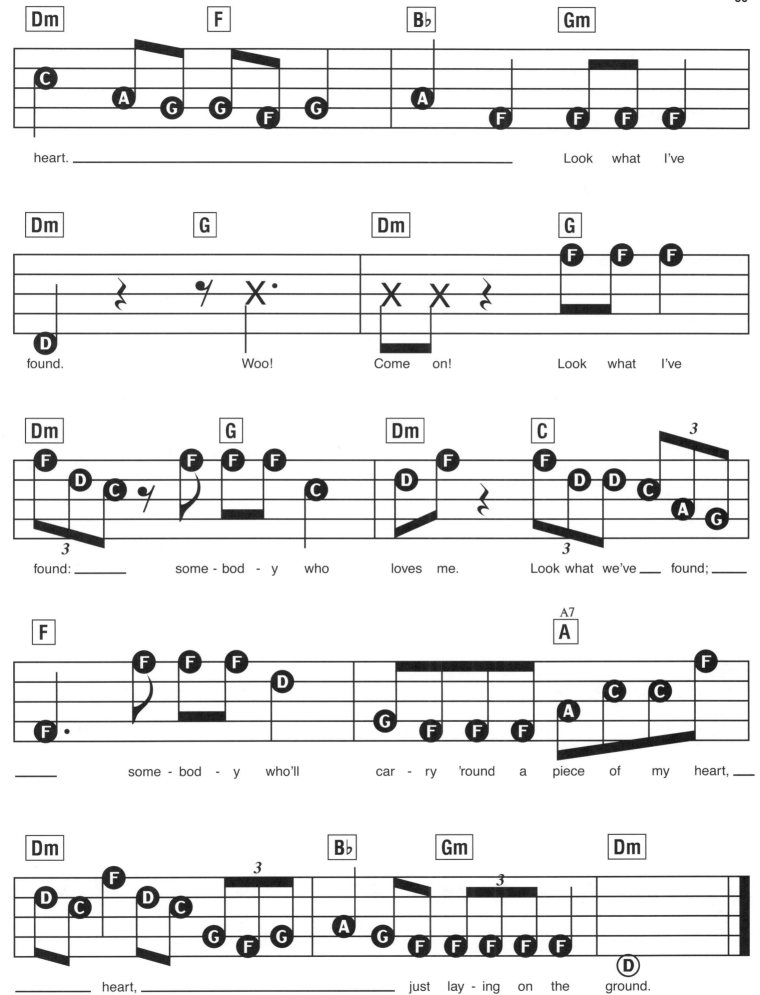

Maybe It's Time
from A STAR IS BORN

Registration 4
Rhythm: Folk

Words and Music by
Michael Isbell

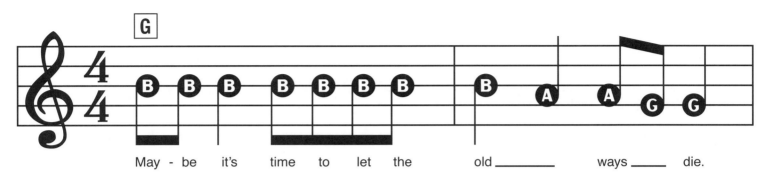

Maybe it's time to let the old _____ ways _____ die.

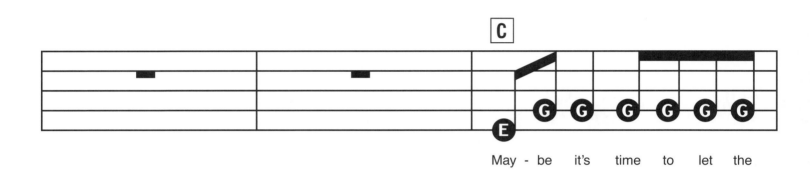

Maybe it's time to let the

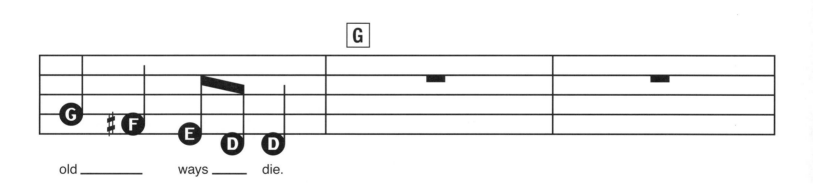

old _____ ways _____ die.

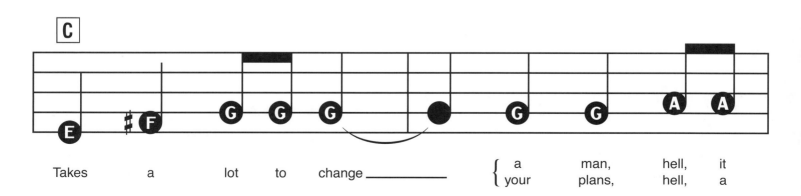

Takes a lot to change _____ { a man, hell, it
your plans, hell, a

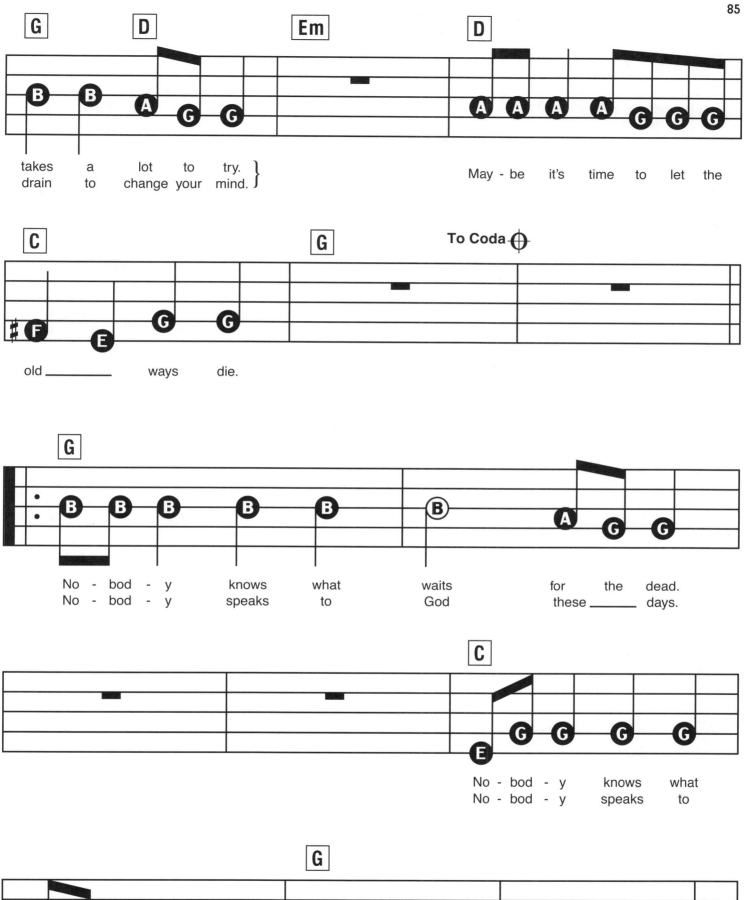

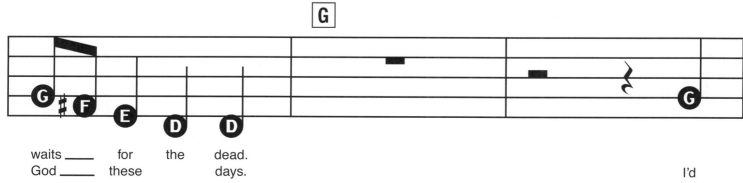

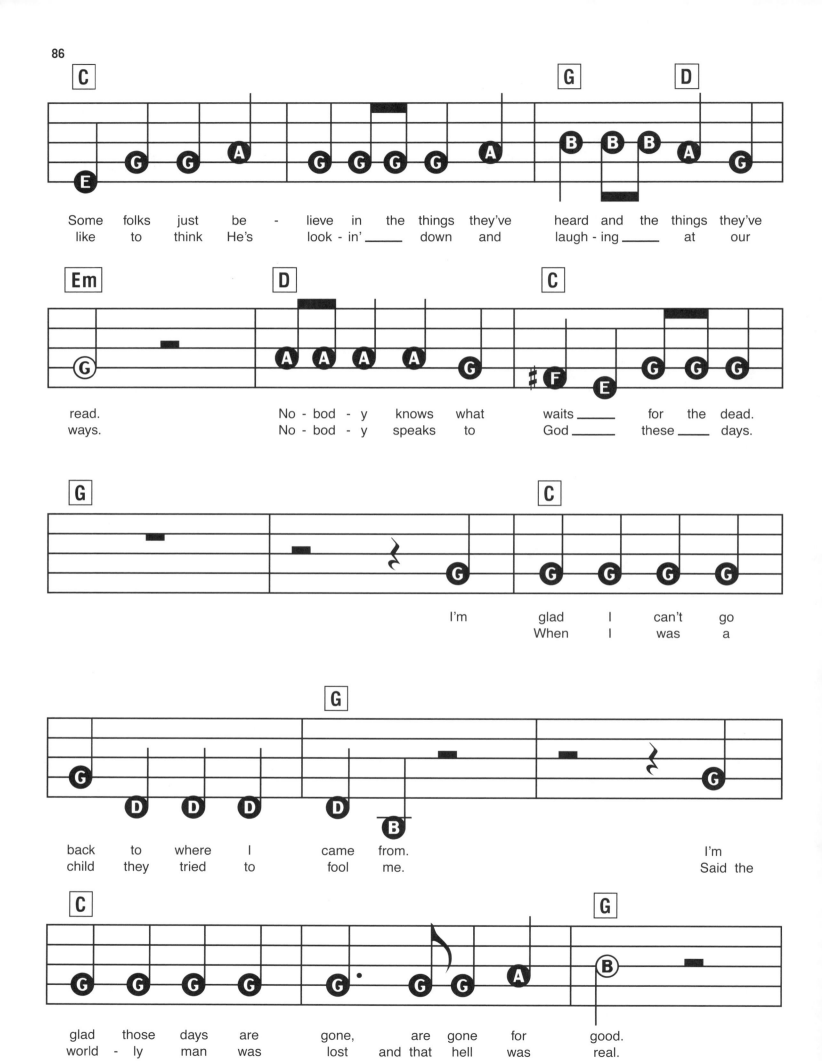

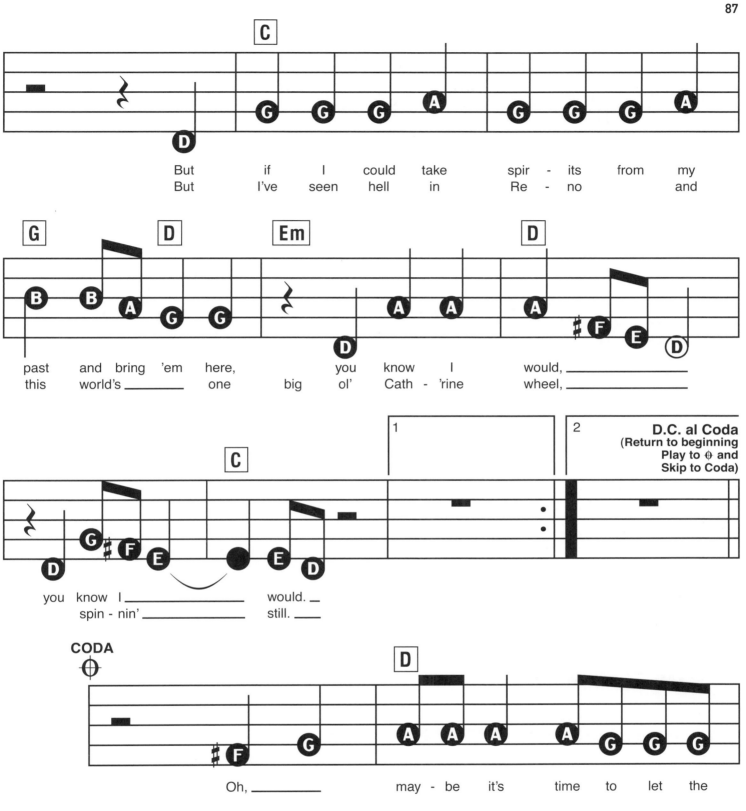

But   if   I   could   take   spir - its   from   my
But   I've seen hell   in   Re - no   and

past   and bring 'em   here,   you know   I   would, _____
this   world's _____ one   big ol' Cath - 'rine wheel, _____

1

2   **D.C. al Coda**
(Return to beginning
Play to ⊕ and
Skip to Coda)

you know I _____ would. __
spin - nin' _____ still. ____

CODA

Oh, _____   may - be it's   time   to   let   the

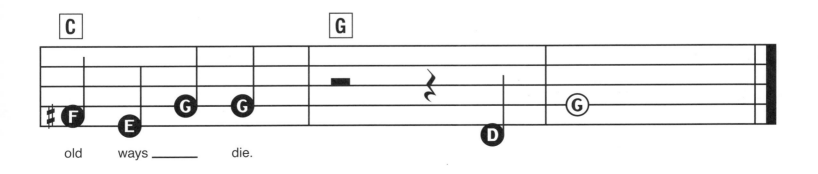

old   ways _____ die.

Shallow
from A STAR IS BORN

Registration 4
Rhythm: Folk

Words and Music by Stefani Germanotta,
Mark Ronson, Andrew Wyatt and Anthony Rossomando

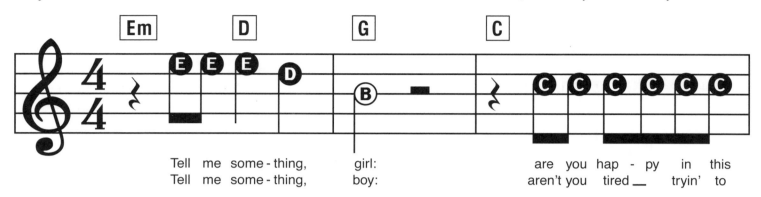

Tell me some-thing, girl: are you hap-py in this
Tell me some-thing, boy: aren't you tired — tryin' to

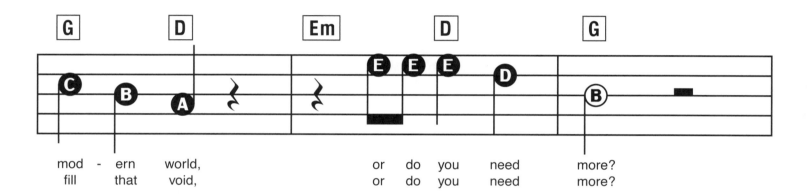

mod-ern world, or do you need more?
fill that void, or do you need more?

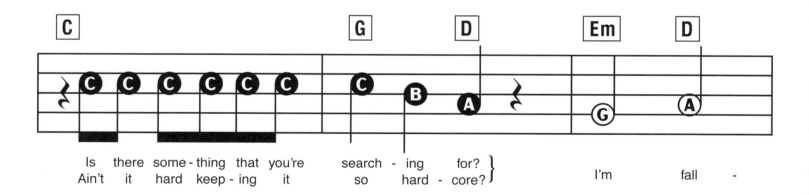

Is there some-thing that you're search-ing for? ⎫ I'm fall -
Ain't it hard keep-ing it so hard-core? ⎭

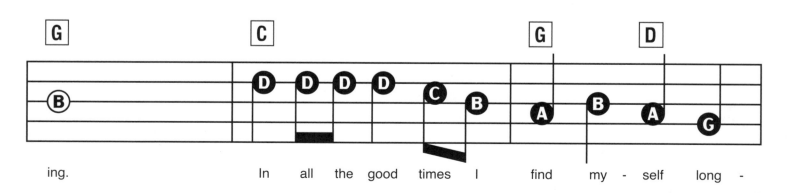

ing. In all the good times I find my-self long -

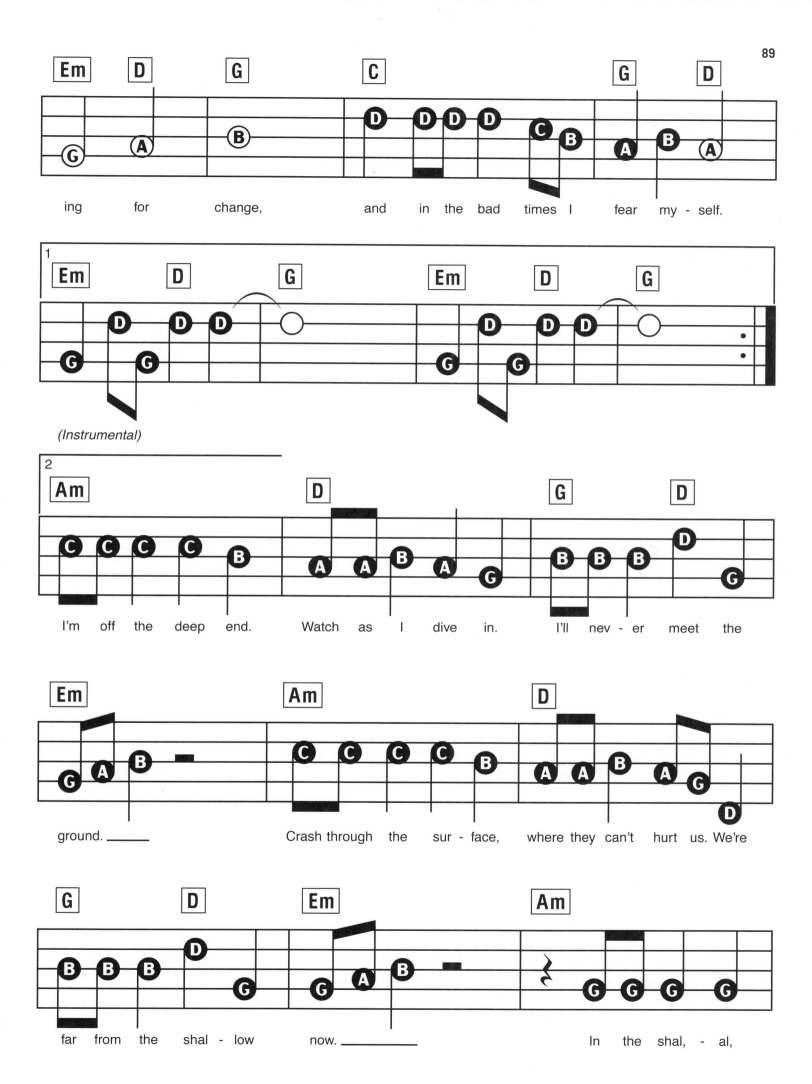

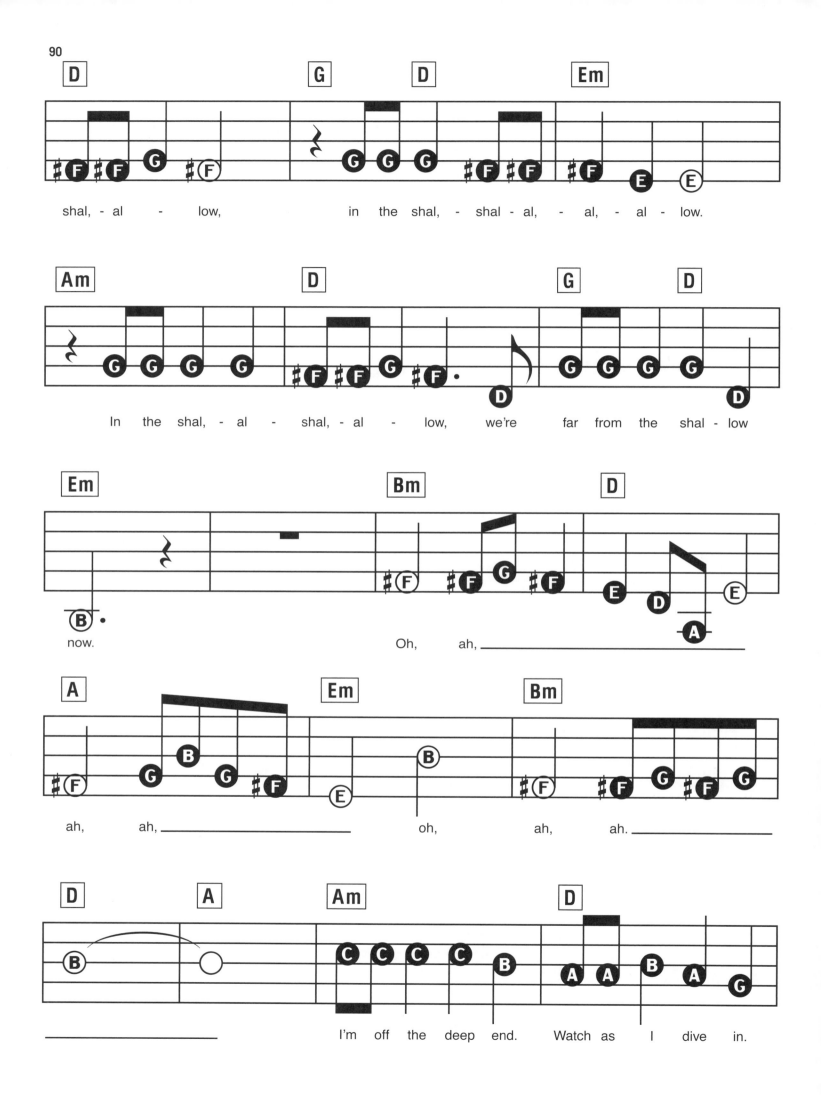

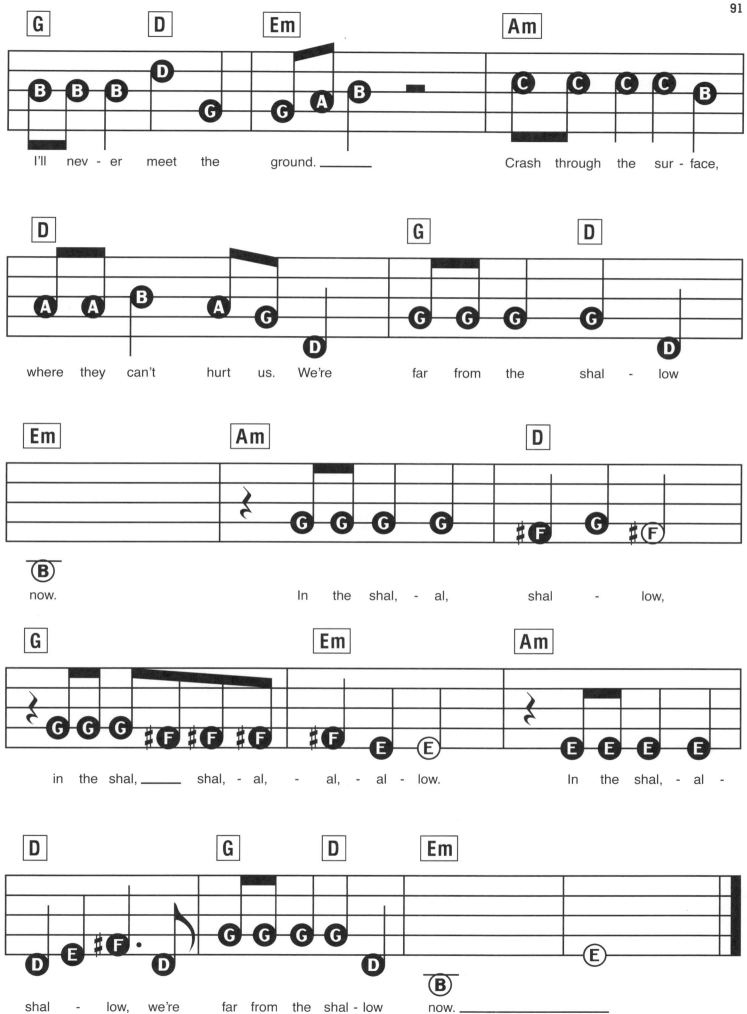

FOR ORGANS, PIANOS & ELECTRONIC KEYBOARDS

E-Z PLAY® TODAY PUBLICATIONS

The E-Z Play® Today songbook series is the shortest distance between beginning music and playing fun! Check out this list of highlights and visit www.halleonard.com for a complete listing of all volumes and songlists.

HAL•LEONARD®

Prices, contents, and availability subject to change without notice.